Judy Bouley takes us into the fascinating world of casting showing her compassion as much as her ability to spot talent. She goes to the ends of the earth to find the right actor for the part.
　　Peter Weir, Director

I first worked with Judy Bouley in 1995 on a film called Outbreak, directed by Wolfgang Petersen. I quickly realized that I could not worry about the casting of local actors and that I was in good hands. We became fast friends based on mutual interests. Judy's casting lends authenticity to the film. Her taste and judgement has enhanced all the projects she's worked on.
　　Jane Jenkins, Legendary Casting Director

About the Author

Judith Bouley works as a casting director in Hollywood and around the world. Born in the U.S., Judy spent her childhood in Japan, where she developed a love of people, cultures, and languages. Those interests, combined with her passion for film, make her career as a casting director part of her DNA. Judy is grateful for the opportunities she's had to work with fascinating people from whom she's learned so much. Judy lives in Hollywood.

Casting Glances

Judith Bouley

Casting Glances

Olympia Publishers
London

www.olympiapublishers.com
OLYMPIA PAPERBACK EDITION

A CIP catalogue record for this title is
available from the British Library.

ISBN: 978-1-83543-128-3

This book is a memoir. No names have been changed, no characters
invented, no events fabricated.

First Published in 2024

Olympia Publishers
Tallis House
2 Tallis Street
London
EC4Y 0AB

Printed in Great Britain

Dedication

For John. My emotional scaffolding. My true north.

"And then there are those we meet, that we barely know, that will tell you a word, a sentence, give you a minute, a half hour, and change the course of your life." – Victor Hugo

"Something that might seem fragile—words arranged on a page—turns out to be indestructible." – Pablo Neruda

Acknowledgments

My love and grateful thanks to:
My amazing brother Mark and my sister of the heart, Diane.
My forever sister, Sandi.
My bonus sister, Cathy.
Kelly, my baby sister.
Chad and Chloe, my family. My nieces and nephews I'm closest
to: Clay, Jessica, Beckett, and Brittan.
Paigey: my heart.
Judy Bernstein: my mentor and shining example.
Jane Jenkins: legendary casting director, potter, and my forever
friend.
Andy Weltman: my producing partner in crime.
My heroes: Duncan Henderson and Peter Weir.
My comrades: Joni Levin and Keith Clarke.
My Rock: Blake Z. Larson.
My additional sister, Karin Babbit.
Susan Zachary and Reyna Clare: Two more of my dear friends.
And whoever you are, wherever you are…you must create. The
world needs your voice.

Tom Hanks Needs Elves!

"The thing about trains is...it doesn't matter where they're going. What matters is deciding to get on."
– Tom Hanks, Conductor on *The Polar Express*

The phone rings in my casting office at Culver Studios. I pick up to hear the producer say, "Morning, Jude. Listen, Bob wants to see you as soon as possible. We need elves."

"Who doesn't?" I reply.

"Come to his office as soon as possible. Bob needs to talk to you about the final scene."

"Yes, sir. I'm heading down now."

I go to my assistant's office to tell them I'll be with the director for a while then walk through the lot to Bob's office, which is a *very* nice motorhome. This isn't his real office; it's his mini-office close to our stage so Bob can easily get to the actors once the assistant director lets him know the lights and camera are set and they are ready for Bob. His mobile office is decked out with a full living room, a large screen monitor, a DVD player, fresh flowers. The fully stocked fridge holds wine, champagne, beer, Perrier, fancy cheeses, crudité, and fruit. There is a huge box of Godiva chocolates next to the cappuccino maker. The large bedroom is good for naps, and the bathroom is good for what bathrooms are good for.

I knock and enter Bob's trailer to find him looking at computer drawings of elves. Some look sweet, some look goofy, some look drunk. They all wear pointy red hats.

"Hey, Jude," Bob says, giving me a hug. "Let's talk elves."

"You know elves are fake right, Bob?" I laugh. "I knew that when I was six"—he just looks at me, so I get serious—"I assumed the plan was to use little people for the elves," I said, "and to computer-generate them to create thousands of the little guys."

"We will, but I need you to find the acrobats or gymnasts or whoever you find who can make the motion we need to bring the elves to life. These elves are serious about making toys. They live for Christmas. Their entire life is serving Santa Claus, the big guy. Oh, and partying. Elf-ing around is all they know. They can't actually do anything else. They're kind of like a film crew," Bob says, laughing.

"Let's get Cirque du Soleil people…acrobats flying through the air, doing backward flips, tossing each other around. Let's get a guy we can shoot out of a cannon. I need a kid acrobat too, say ten to twelve years old. We'll shoot their motion. Visual effects will lay over the images of the elves onto their movement. Any questions?"

"Nope," I reply.

"Push this to the top of your list, Jude. I'll need these guys for rehearsal in two weeks."

"This will be fun to cast. And Bob, I won't let you or Santa down."

Bob is Robert Zemeckis, the Oscar-winning writer, director, and producer. A protégé of Steven Spielberg, Bob has directed some of the biggest blockbusters of the past few decades. His resume is incredible: *Back to the Future, Death Becomes Her, Who Framed Roger Rabbit, Romancing the Stone, Contact, Castaway,* and a long list of others. *Forrest Gump,* for which Bob

14

and Tom Hanks and a host of others won Oscars, is a cinematic classic. I've been in the trenches with Bob on four of his films, *Contact*, *Castaway*, *What Lies Beneath*, and now, *The Polar Express*. If Bob wants elves, he'll get elves! I head back to my office by way of the cafeteria.

Being on any movie lot is a surreal experience. With four films in production besides ours, the cafeteria is packed. I walk through a throng of 1950s Pan American Airline beauties with bouffant hair, pearls, and shoes that look like they hurt. A green-haired zombie dressed in a black leather cape smeared with blood orders the seared mahi tuna platter, rare, from the grill cook. At the 'coffee corner,' two armored Roman soldiers are in line behind Jesus who orders a macchiato and a plain croissant, which I'm hoping he will multiply and feed to the hungry.

The Polar Express is a feature film based on a beautifully written and illustrated children's book of the same name. Author Chris Van Allsburg tells the story of a young boy who boards a magical train headed to the North Pole on Christmas Eve. The child, who does not believe in Christmas, takes a terrifying journey through the tender terrain of self-exploration and finally arrives at the magic and wonder of those who believe in Christmas.

Tom Hanks stars in this $200 million all-digital motion/performance capture film. *Ours* is the first film of its kind. Tom plays six roles: the narrator, the train conductor, the father, the hobo, Scrooge the puppet, and Santa Claus. Bob wants more than animation; he wants the characters in the film to look almost human... *'like putting the soul of a live person into a virtual character.'* This has never been done before, and it's taking hundreds of talented, dedicated people to pull it off.

Performance capture, or motion capture, as it is popularly

15

called, is often shortened to the nickname, 'mo-cap.' In simple terms, special cameras record the motion of the actor through the use of numerous sensors transmitting information to computers. The actor wears a skintight black body suit, like the wetsuits surfers wear. On the suit, sensors resembling small, white round balls are attached at strategic points on the actor's face and body.

On *The Polar Express,* we have thirty-six cameras placed all around the set, digitally recording, many times per second, a 360-degree view of the actor's movements. That digital information is collected via the sensors and then fed to a team of computer wizards who transfer the actors' movements to a 3D model. Through the magic of visual effects (VFX), our handful of elves will be reproduced into thousands; some sweet, some goofy, some drunk…all with pointy red hats.

I spend the morning researching local gymnasts and acrobats, then wander down to Stage three to watch Tom Hanks doing his camera tests. Sitting in his director's chair, Bob watches Tom on a video monitor as he goes through his initial scene as the conductor on *The Polar Express*. Surrounding Bob is Steve Starkey, his producer; Ken Ralston, the VFX genius who created the performance capture process Bob needs. Also in attendance is the Assistant Director whose job it is to carry out Bob's commands.

Once everyone and everything is in place, the AD lets the director know we are ready to shoot.

"And…action," Bob calls out. Tom strikes a T Pose then stands next to empty space, which he pretends is a train. He calls the children to board the train. As he looks at his gold pocket watch he shouts, "ALL ABOARD! I said, ALL ABOARD! Let's go! Tick tock tick tock. No time to waste. ALL ABOARD *THE POLAR EXPRESS*!"

"Cut," says Bob.

"Cut," the AD repeats.

"And T Pose, please, Tom." Tom assumes the position, which means he is standing straight with his arms extended to each side, like the letter T. Essentially, the T Pose is like Jesus on the cross, if Jesus were wearing a wetsuit with white sensors pasted all over his body. This marks the end of the scene. Tom walks over, sits in his chair, and watches playback on the monitor. All the guys laugh, pleased with what they shot, and the AD calls the lunch break.

I walk back to my office, pondering. We're making Christmas. We need elves. Where's the best place for me to start? I remember that my associate, Tom Gustafson, had briefly trained at San Francisco Circus Center. Tom is young, handsome, pork pie hat hip, well-educated, funny, and crazy talented. Now a director in his own right, Tom had worked as my associate on two great films. He spent a year with me in Baja, California, on Peter Weir's epic film, *Master and Commander,* and eight months with me in Chicago on *The Road to Perdition*, also starring Tom Hanks.

"I dial," he answers. "Tommy, I need elves for Bob Z's new film. Didn't you go to circus school in San Francisco at one time?"

"Yeah...for two months...and now I'm scared to death of clowns. They're creepy."

"OK. That's weird. Did you learn anything else besides clowning when you were there?"

"Yeah. I took beginning acrobatics, wire walking. You start with the balance beam then work up to walking on the wire. I played on the trapeze and trained with some clowns. They scared the shit out of me."

"That's hilarious. Anything else?"

"The Circus Center is exactly where you'll find your elves."

San Francisco Circus Center is a world-renowned training ground for acrobats and gymnasts. Classes include: acrobatics, contortion, juggling, clowning, flying trapeze, wire walking, pretzeling their bodies, and anything else up in the air, upside down, backward, and seemingly impossible, which, when you think about it, is exactly what you need in an elf!

The director and head trainer of the Circus Center is Master Lu Yi, a small, amazingly fit Chinese man in his early seventies. He brings fifty years of his extraordinary experience to the Center. Vice President of the Chinese Acrobats Association, Master Lu Yi was also a star performer and director of China's celebrated Nanjing Acrobatic Troupe.

After a long phone call explaining my elf task, Master Lu Yi invites me to spend the afternoon interviewing and filming his students. Ranging in age from six to sixty, the acrobats' experience runs from none to years of performing with Cirque du Soleil.

Heading up to San Francisco Circus School, I drive along the Pacific Coast of California and once again realize that my job comes with amazing moments. I watch dolphins jump and whales breech, I remember flying to Montevideo on *Evita* for dinner with a famous Argentinian actress, and on *Master and Commander*, I climbed the rigging of our tall ship as we sailed away from port in Ensenada to do our helicopter shots of the ship gliding through the ocean. Russell Crowe was at the helm. Magical moments indeed.

At Circus School, in a huge wooden gymnasium, I have a blast filming folks as they fly through the air, walk on wires and

18

stilts, swing on a trapeze, ride backward on unicycles, make pretzels out of their body parts and literally clown around. I know immediately Bob has to have these athletes. Bingo! One-stop shopping, and I find the elves, including the young boy, who I film being tossed back and forth, very high up in the air, between two male gymnasts. *His parents let him do this?* I think. Clearly, the boy was enjoying himself.

At the end of the day, thrilled with all the work, I pack up my gear and bow profusely, thanking Master Lu Yi for his kind help. "Yes. You are very welcome," he replies. And then, "Before you go, would you like to fly on the trapeze?"

"Well, YES!" I say. And so, without thinking it through, in short order, I am in a huge room with a high trapeze, being outfitted in a leather harness as a gaggle of people watch me.

At the Circus Center, for a small fee, adults and children can pay to fly on the trapeze. A handful of people, waiting for their turn, watch me as I start up the ladder. I decide to look brave even though I am envisioning the fall to my death due to a broken harness and a rip in the net. I am certain I will be the first dead person at the Circus Center. But I said I'm doing this so by God, wise or unwise, I am doing this. I've been told numerous times, by numerous people: family, friends, colleagues, and especially lovers that I'm stubborn. I like to think of myself as tenacious.

And here, let me just say a word about one of the most frightening parts of the whole escapade…the slow climb up the world's highest, skinniest ladder. Steel steps, cold under my sweaty hands, go straight up. As I climb, I feel I'm going into outer space. The scent of talcum powder and body odor has me a bit queasy. *Please God, I pray thee, keep me from vomiting on the crowd.*

After climbing the ridiculously tall ladder, I arrive at a

ridiculously tiny platform, really just a piece of two-by-four plank, about three feet long. And thirty feet up in the air.

"Keep going and whatever you do," a voice says. "Don't look down." *Not a chance of that,* I think. A young, blonde acrobat, with zero body fat and arms the size of my thighs, receives me at the top of the ladder. "I'm Eric," he announces. *I don't care.* I think. *Just get me down from here immediately.*

"Hi, Eric. I'm Judy," I say, enthusiastically.

"OK, now just hold onto me, Judy, and inch yourself out onto the plank. I'll give you the bar of the trapeze and when you're ready, I'll give you a little push to start your swing, OK?"

NO! I think.

"OK," I mumble.

"Good. Now, remember, there is a very sturdy net to catch you if you fall. It's best if you don't look down, OK? Just grip the bar, pump your legs like you're on a swing, keep your focus straight ahead, and enjoy the ride. You ready?"

Fuck no! I think.

"READY!" I shout. Like a loud, people-pleasing elf.

"Off you go!" says Eric, and pushes me into the air. Into outer space. Into nothingness.

I death grip the steel bar of the trapeze and just kind of hang there, forty feet up in the air. Like a stalactite. "Pump your legs, Judy!" he shouts. So I do. Up and down, slowly at first. Then ramping up. I pump as if my life depended on it, and finally, I'm covering some ground. As it were.

Flying through the air, swinging back and forth, pumping harder, going higher and higher, giggling with exhilaration and less fear, it dawns on me that I am flying on a trapeze! I feel strong and scared and slightly graceful. And I have *absolutely* no idea how to get back down on terra firma. So I keep pumping.

20

After a short while, Eric says, loudly, "OK, Judy. Drop!" And I think, *Are you on crack? I'm thirty feet up in the air! There's not a chance in hell I'm letting go.* "DROP!" he repeats. But I don't. We rally for another twenty seconds, and then Eric says, "DROP NOW, JUDY!" I execute three more vigorous swings because now I don't want to get off the trapeze. I love this freedom of flying. I throw my heart over the bar and my body follows.

And then with one enormous inhale, I open my clenched hands, release the cold bar of the trapeze, and fall through the air.

How's that for a metaphor? Filmmaking and sometimes falling in love are very much like this.

The only difference is…with Circus School, you get a net.

Fair Winds, Open Hearts, Safe Journey

"You must give me the entire human community, the best and the worst of men...and we must love them for their faults."
– Peter Weir, Director *Master and Commander*

"Anybody want to go to Mexico with Russell Crowe?" I shouted to the masses sitting on mauve padded chairs in Ballroom II of the San Diego Marriott.

"Ahoy matey, that would be me!" answered a middle-aged bald bloke who never missed a meal. He wore huge loops in his pierced ears and a bright green parrot on his right shoulder...dressed as a pirate, that is, if it was Halloween and you were six and your mom bought you a pirate get-up at any drug store. A button-less beige shirt showing more of his chest than was necessary was tucked into dirty muslin pants which were tucked into black leather, gold-buckled knee-high boots. A silver sword hung at his side.

This is gonna be rugged, I thought and turned back to the crowd.

February 2002 was my first open casting call for the Peter Weir film, *Master and Commander, the Far Side of the World.* We'd advertised well in the southern California newspapers, radio, and television networks, and close to eighteen hundred people responded.

My staff and I were well-prepared. Our advertised time to begin was eleven a.m. We arrived at eight a.m. to set up our room only to discover a line already snaked around the building.

Two names produced all the interest: Director Peter Weir and Actor Russell Crowe.

As my staff handed out applications for all to complete, I walked down the line welcoming people as I scanned faces, body language...feeling the energy of the hopefuls as I began my search for fifty-five men and four boys who would become part of Captain Aubrey's/Russell Crowe's crew for this feature film to begin shooting in June at Fox Studios in Baja, California.

We let one hundred people at a time inside the ballroom where everyone completed their applications. In the front of the room, on a microphone, I explained, with great enthusiasm, the story of our film, a seafaring journey set in 1806, and what an adventure it would be shooting for five months in the water tank at Fox Baja Studio in Rosarito where our construction department was building a tall ship, circa 1796. We would also shoot at sea. I explained that at Peter Weir's request, the studio had purchased from the Rhode Island Maritime Museum an authentic tall ship, built in the late 1700s.

A crew would sail it down the Atlantic Ocean, through the Panama Canal, and up the Pacific Ocean to finally anchor in Ensenada. We would use that ship for shots at sea from helicopters or camera boats loaded with elaborate cranes and cameras.

"So if you get seasick," I said, "this is not the movie for you."

After I spoke, the men went to the photo stations in the back of the room where my staff photographed each person and collected their application.

On the walls, I had posted research photos of tall ships,

23

nautical maps, and portraits of sailors of all races, from the late eighteen hundreds, to further paint the picture of what we would create on film. There were pictures of Russell Crowe and of our visionary director, Peter Weir, along with a partial list of Peter's credits: *Dead Poet's Society, The Truman Show, Witness, Green Card, Gallipoli, and more.* Russell Crowe's included: *A Beautiful Mind, Gladiator, and LA Confidential.*

The last thing I said into the mic is, "Thank you for your interest in our film. To be frank, it's a d*on't-call-us, we'll-call-you situation.*"

As my staff photographed the crowd, I retired to a private room for quick interviews with the small group of people I'd selected for the next step.

My eyes scanned the audience. I had already seen some great candidates: a broken-nosed, thin as a paperclip Irish lad, a shaggy-haired, blonde third-grader, and his fourteen-year-old brother.

I asked those I'd quietly selected, a touch to their shoulder, a quick hello, to meet with me after the room cleared. About fifteen of them stayed, and my sifting process began. As we talked, I decided who I wanted to audition the following week and explained that together we would improve a scene in which they would ask His Majesty's Captain for a job or try to escape from being pressed into service. Their choice, and they were not to tell me which they would choose. I would discover that at their audition. I asked them to create their backstory (the story of their character) to make their character authentic. My assistant organized individual audition appointments for the following week at a suite in the same hotel. By then, the room had emptied, and the next group filed in. I returned to the front of the room and greeted the next one hundred hopefuls. "Anybody wanna go to

Mexico with Russell Crowe?"

By eight p.m., I was hoarse, exhausted, and ready for a cocktail.

On that particular Saturday in February, I gave my speech eighteen times. My staff booked over two hundred men and boys for auditions in San Diego alone. From February to May, we held casting calls in Baja, Los Angeles, Santa Cruz, Vancouver, and Toronto. In all, we processed close to a thousand hopefuls to cast fifty-five main crew for Her Majesty's ship, sixty 'B' crew for our battle scenes, and two hundred and fifty French sailors.

Then I saddled up to go to the next town. Rinse and repeat.

On the Way to Mexico I Swung by Sudan!

And now to auditions. Next, please.
– Judy Bouley, Casting Director, Author

"Who's next?" I say this to my smart, loyal casting associate, Tom Gustafson, who is running the camera. We are crammed into a tiny, airless room at the San Diego Alliance for African Refugees in search of African men to play sailors on Russell Crowe's crew for *Master and Commander*.

"Benjamin Ajak," Tom replies. "He's just arrived to America from Kenya. He's a Sudanese refugee."

Tom escorts in a stunning young man who is 6'5", with glorious blue-black skin like a Masai warrior and a seductive smile. At nineteen years old, Benjamin has tired, angry eyes and fierce dignity. I'm already in love.

"Thank you for coming, Benjamin," I begin.

"No, it is for me to thank you," he replies and takes my small hand in his huge one.

"Benjamin, I can't comprehend what you've been through in your life. I'm so grateful you're in America now. We are a better country now."

"Yes," he replies. "It is a blessing to be here. Now I am a free man. I want to work in a Hollywood movie!"

"Benjamin, I know little about your story. I only know that you came from horrific violence and lived many years in a refugee camp."

And Benjamin tells me his unbelievable story.

Benjamin's father was the Chief of their village in southern Sudan. He was called upon to settle disputes among the villagers. He owned forty goats and warded off lions. His good wife raised Benjamin, age five, to be a strong and resourceful boy. One day as Benjamin tended the goats, the armed Janjaweed, Arab horsemen, attacked and torched their village. Benjamin saw his mother and father murdered.

Benjamin soon found his cousins, Alepho, age seven, and Benson, eleven in the stream of terrified boys. The cousins became part of the thousands of boys who walked across the parching Sudanese desert, almost twelve hundred miles, into Ethiopia and eventually to Kakuma Refugee Camp in Kenya to escape the bloody civil war in their country. This mass of brave children survived massacres and starvation. Some were eaten by crocodiles in the Gilo River. Benjamin, Alepho, and Benson drank their own urine and sucked stones to stay alive.

Most boys walked barefoot and naked through the treacherous desert. Thousands died in the dirt. They were called the Lost Boys.

"OK, Benjamin. Are you ready to begin?" He nods yes. "Great. Sit on the chair in front of the camera and pretend you have come to tell the captain why you want to sail with him on his ship, the HMS Surprise. I will play the part of the captain. Pretend you are a man who has left his young family back in Africa and likely you will never see them again. Can you do that?"

Benjamin looks directly at me and says, "I will not need to pretend that."

"Boy, why are you here before me?" I begin.

"Sir, I must take a job."

"Have you sailed before?"

"No, sir."

"Boy, can you cook?"

"Small things, sir."

"Do you believe in God the Almighty?"

Benjamin goes silent, and then..."I AM God." Tom and I exchange a quick glance.

I get back into character. "Can you shoot a musket?"

"Yes."

"Can you kill a man if I order you to?"

Benjamin turns his head to stare straight at me. "Yes. I can kill a man. I know of these things." And I see that he has slipped out of character and at that moment is back in war-torn Sudan. I change tact.

"What is your native language, son?"

"Dinka," he replies.

"Great. Please sit on the floor as if you are sitting on the bow of the ship, alone on a moonless night. Just you, the black sky, and the ocean. I want you to sing a song in Dinka, any song. Sing a lullaby, or anything else that tells how you feel as you sail away forever from your family."

Benjamin doesn't move. He folds his arms across his chest, like the Dinka warrior he is. Embarrass. He won't sing.

"Stand next to Tom at the camera, Benjamin. Look through the camera lens and watch me." Then I take his place in front of the camera. I sit on the floor, pull my knees to my chest, wrap my arms around them, and softly sing in Japanese. Because I can.

It's a sad song and my accent is true. I sing believing that while I serve this good captain.

I will never again see my family. Benjamin stares at me.

28

Finish. I wordlessly get up and motion for him to sit in front of the camera on the bow of the ship.

Benjamin wails in Dinka as Tom and I fight back tears.

At that moment, I knew Benjamin's audition would be the first I would show Peter.

I did. Ten bars into the song, Peter turned to me and said, "He's in the movie. Very good. You've already set the bar quite high, Judy. OK, who's next?"

Chase, a ten-year-old fourth-grader and his fourteen-year-old brother, Christian, were cast as powder monkeys, the lads who run gunpowder to the sailors. Georgios, a middle-aged Greek banker from Vancouver played the role of a diver called Old Sponge. The crew fleshed out with a university photography teacher, an Irish musician, Australian and American seasoned tall ship sailors, an apple farmer, two Sudanese refugees, a German holistic healer, and twin brothers from Mexico, with the coolest noses I'd ever seen and many more.

A casting director in Poland submitted a tape with over three hundred Polish men. From that, Peter and I selected a dozen men to import. Among them curly-haired Marian, a social worker by trade, Pawel, a devout student of Buddhism working on his law degree, Radek, a popular actor from Warsaw theatre.

Five months later, our jigsaw puzzle of fifty-five souls was painstakingly assembled.

The night before our first day of filming, Peter and our amazing producer, Duncan Henderson held a grog party for cast and crew. As we raised our glasses Peter thanked everyone for their tireless work preparing the film and reminded us that we were paying tribute to the courageous men who, on a tall ship in 1806, served the Queen of England, battled the French, and found in each of them their greatest selves.

With three 'huzzahs' we said our goodnights and walked into a saffron sunset. I held back, watching the guileless men and boys who, for five months, under Peter's direction would tell the story of intrigue, fear, and sheer bravery. We had created a family.

When I began casting for *Master and Commander,* Peter gave me my marching orders.

"Judy, you must give me men from the entire human community: sailors, soldiers, musicians, carpenters, fathers, thieves, men pressed into service. The best and the worst of men. And we should love them for their faults." I wrote that on a post-it note which lived on my bulletin board. I have it still.

After six months of prep, meeting thousands of hopefuls, it was time to start shooting. So we did. Our dailies (film we watched that we shot the day before making sure there were no hairs on the camera lens). Russell Crowe behaved himself mostly until one day, when we were filming at sea.

Pods of dolphins play in the Pacific as the sun scorches through square muslin sails of our tall ship. This is the ship our construction crew built, an exact replica of the 1786 frigate purchased, for eight hundred thousand dollars by Fox Studio for the film. The Rose left Rhode Island, traveled through the Panama Canal and was harbored in Ensenada, ready to be taken out to sea when Peter films scenes of the ship sailing. We shot with a camera ship mounted on a helicopter. Heaven. The constructed ship lives in the water tank at Fox Baja, the tank which was built for the filming of *Titanic.*

Today the wooden deck is packed with the hand-picked human community that is the HMS Surprise: sailors of all ranks. We are filming this day with full complement, men and boys ages ten to fifty, costumed in handmade hemp uniforms each detail specific to their rank or particular duty: midshipmen, powder monkeys, the cook's mate. Gregorian chants play loudly as most of the men stand in silence gazing anywhere but at each other. A small group of men and boys rehearse stitching their dead mates into muslin sheaths. This is the day we bury our dead at sea. Peter Weir takes the microphone and encourages everyone to stay in character, advising that soon Russell will arrive on the water taxi, climb the gangplank, and join us on deck.

Russell Crowe is late again. We wait. And wait. Make-up artists swirl around as fast as they can touching up melting make-up, re-applying dirt and blood to faces and fingernails. My crew and I hand out bottled waters. Gregorian chant continues.

An hour later, Peter is told Russell is on his way. The director reminds each of the sailors of the solemnity of this afternoon's scene. As a brotherhood, they bury their dead.

When Russell finally arrives he appears not as a movie star but completely in character as the great Captain Aubrey who has mustered his strength this day to lead his men in burying their own. Before he begins his speech Russell asks Peter for the microphone and turns to face the crowd. "My good friend and great actor Richard Harris died today. As we do our work this afternoon let us remember him. Let us remember all those we have lost."

And with that, he took his place on deck, Peter calls action and Captain Aubrey gives his entire speech in one unmistakably earnest take.

"Michael Alfred Doudle, John Henry Allen, Joseph Nagle. We therefore commit their bodies to the deep, looking for the resurrection of the body, when the sea shall give up her dead. Amen." And then he leads the men in prayer: "Our father, which art in heaven…"

Around the lot, I became known as Mama Bouley. I was dubbed so by Benjamin Ajak, one of the Sudanese sailors. "You have so many people to take care of their hearts," Benjamin said to me one day as I was watching him in the make-up chair—the artist dirtying his nails and teeth transforming him into a sailor from 1806. My mornings included greeting my 'babies' in the sailor's den each morning as the men ate their breakfast and prepared for the long day's shooting schedule. I believe it is critical to acknowledge each of them—to thank them for what I know they will give Peter that day. It's my job to remind them they are a precious part of the whole. In the end, I believe that's what we all want to be—part of something bigger than ourselves.

As a wrap gift, our sailors were given a gorgeous photo album by Russell Crowe. The exterior was made of exotic wood from New Zealand. From the producers, they received a t-shirt that had sails representing all the countries of our cast and crew. I gave them a beautiful photo I shot in the tank…our tall ship against the Pacific Ocean and a soft blue sky.

Dear Ones,

As we are coming to the end of this film, there is so much I want to say to each one of you.

I am proud of you for many things: long days, harsh nights, your fierce commitment to Peter and me being thrashed about during the storm scenes, out at sea, and on the gun deck. You worked when you were dog tired and ill.

Mostly, I am proud of how you became a true brotherhood, supporting and caring for each other.

You honored Peter's request to pay reverence to the men you were portraying by becoming true sailors.

Your brotherhood, now on film, will soon be out in the universe.

And that, my dear ones, is what moves the world forward. Thank you for unfurling the sails to help Peter and all of us on this journey to the Far Side of the World.

Fair winds, safe journey...open hearts and minds.

Love, Mama Bouley

Wani
Master and Commander, 2002

Well, this is a fine mess you've gotten us into, Miss Bouley!
– Duncan Henderson, amazing man, producer, and
unforgettable friend.

If you're planning to smuggle a young African refugee, say one under the age of twelve, over the Mexican border into America on a school day, I strongly urge you to pack snacks.

Eleven-year-old Wani Chol and I were stuck in an endless line of overheating cars snaking forward one nanosecond every three minutes as the temperature gauge inside my rented white Ford Taurus read ninety-two degrees. We'd left the studio in Rosarito early this morning heading for San Diego. I just wanted to get the kid home for the weekend with his family. Back to real life. He needed a break from the set, the sailors, and the pool table in the sailor's den where the children we cast would hang out after filming and completing their daily lessons with their studio teacher.

I met Wani in San Diego in his home, in my search for boys, ages nine to fourteen, to play 'powder monkeys,' the young boys employed as black powder runners on sailing warships in the early 1800s. Since Wani wasn't needed for filming until the following Tuesday, it made sense to let him have a weekend at home then return to Mexico on Monday to shoot his final scene.

34

That was the plan, and we headed for the border.

Tijuana, Mexico. The busiest border in the world, as twenty-four lanes of cars move, or don't, out of and into America or Mexico.

Wooden stalls, blankets laid on the side of the road, or an old piece of cardboard under an umbrella serve as the center of commerce on the Mexican side of the border where you can haggle for a reduced price on a Spongebob pinata, woven baskets, jute hammocks, glazed pottery donkey statues, lapis silver watchbands, thirty brands of Tequila, and Viagra...no prescription needed!

Wani stared out the car window to see tiny women with hungry babies in makeshift slings wandering up and down, hands outstretched, occasionally collecting a few pesos from strangers. Shoeless, dirty children begged too, their vacant eyes connected with anyone who cared to glance back. Most didn't. Some as young as four threaded through the line of cars selling hot pink ukuleles, Spiderman masks, stale chewing gum, *"Chiclet Senora?"* And Jesus soap on a rope.

"That boy is hungry," Wani said, pointing to one of the dirty children. "I'm hungry too."

I rolled down my window and gave the boy ten pesos. "I know, sweetheart. We'll drive through McDonald's once we're over the border."

Up ahead a wrinkled grandmother dipped thick yellow batter into hot grease then dusted cinnamon and sugar onto long twisted pastries before hanging them on a display rack made of old wire clothes hangers. Wani looked at the pastries then at me.

"Nope," I said. He wiggled in his seat. Sweltering and sick of sitting in bumper-to-bumper traffic, I was determined to get Wani home for a weekend with his family.

35

Approaching the border to cross into America, you first see a red light, ALTO. This is your cue to stop as you wait for the green light so you can inch ahead to the concrete kiosk where a border patrol officer asks to see your papers as he, or she does a quick glance inside your car. If they suspect anything irregular (say drugs or child trafficking) they have you pull your car over and escort you inside a square grey government issue concrete building, to speak to an immigration office. That's where the real fun begins.

I roll down the window and say, "Good morning, sir." To a gum-snapping, sweaty, pockmarked border patrol officer, strapped to a large revolver.

"Papers."

I hand him my American passport and Wani's green card.

"You his mother?"

"No, sir. I'm his guardian. Wani is working with us at Fox Studio in Rosarito."

"On Russell Crowe's new movie." I throw in for good measure, praying he's a fan and saw *Gladiator*.

"Where are his parents?"

"They live in San Diego. That's where we're headed now, sir."

"I don't think so."

"Excuse me?"

"His green card's expired."

"That can't be," I protest. "He went home last weekend without any problem."

"Well, he's not going home today. His green card expired three weeks ago. So pull your car over, miss. You're going to Immigration."

Liquid brown eyes stare up at me. Shoving my hand into my

purse, I come up with wintergreen Tic Tacs. My eyes raise heavenward as I whisper, *"I'm sorry, God...it's the best I can do."*

Seated inside the waiting room for some hours, of the Immigration Department, Wani and I are staring at a dreadful reproduction of a dreadful oil painting of George Bush which replicates him exactly. "Who is he?" Wani asks.

"The President of the United States."

"He looks dumb."

"He is dumb."

"Oh. Then why is he the president?"

"Because half of America is stupid," I reply.

Wani swings his little legs back and forth, alternating; first one then the other making sucking sounds against the frayed maroon plastic covering on the government issue chairs. It sounds like he is continually farting. It's bugging me, but gives me something to focus on besides the dumb president.

We have been staring at this photo since eight a.m. when Wani and I were escorted to Immigration by the gum-smacking Border Patrol guy with the gun who I sensed was not, in his senior year, voted most likely to succeed. He sashayed ahead looking back over his shoulder every three seconds, ready to pounce if we try to make a break for it and vanish behind any number of hot pink clown piñatas hanging from hooks in the congested street market outside Border Patrol.

"Why do they have guns?" Wani whispers.

"Because they're bad guys," I reply. And then think, *Well, that was a stupid thing to say to an eleven-year-old Sudanese refugee who knows first-hand the definition of genocide.*

"Like in the movies?"

"Exactly like in the movies."

37

No such luck for Wani and me. We're in real life—in a stuffy, government waiting room, filled with regular, nice Mexican people just trying to get a one-day pass to drive over the border to spend their hard-earned pesos, which they'll need to change, to stock up at Costco. Who devised a system wherein one has to interview with a uniformed armed officer to be granted the privilege of driving north to purchase a dozen cans of tuna or mayo in bulk?

"I'm hungry," Wani announces, for the third time. Glancing down at his pencil-thin frame, it dawns on me that Wani knows more than any child should about hunger. Half a cup of cornmeal was a good day at the refugee camp in Kakuma, Kenya where Wani and his family called home for over three years.

"Can we go back to the cafeteria and eat with the crew? I want movie lunch."

"*Ah,* yes. Movie lunch." We are spoiled with our catered film crew lunches. A typical day's menu: thick, perfectly grilled rib-eye steaks, fresh catch of the day in parchment paper, apricot fennel Gruyere filo rolls, Mediterranean chicken, ricotta pesto pasta, assorted fancy salads (at least five), fingerling potatoes, orzo, freshly baked bread with crunchy crust, hot fudge sundaes, a banana flambé station, warm chocolate chip and peanut butter cookies. Of course, Wani wanted to go back to the studio and eat with the crew. All he's got is my old TicTacs.

In lieu of eating, Wani resumes the leg swinging. A female officer, thirty-something, in a wrinkle-free beige uniform, black boots, and a holstered revolver scan the room. Her dark eyes settle on me. "OK, miss. Step up to the blue line. You're next."

Wani's eyebrows raise. I tell him to come with me—he's a good visual prop—innocently small, deep blue-black skin, little boy fingers. We hold hands which I think is a nice touch, 'black and white, we are fam-i-ly.' Hey...what a different looking, interesting pair *we* are—notice us, we're special—speed us through your bureaucratic bullshit because we are the most interesting people in your dull, grey lives today and for the foreseeable future.

Standing *precisely* on the blue line I glance at the officer's name badge. Claudia Ramirez. Quickly, I consider whether to address her by her first or last name. Go casual or business? I decide on business.

"Yes, Officer Ramirez," I say. Then deciding peppy is the way to go. "What's the good news?"

"There's a problem with the boy's visa."

"What's the problem?"

"There's an issue with his refugee status."

"OK. What's the issue? Let's fix it!" I say, still peppy.

"Well, it's not that easy. The proper paperwork was submitted by the boy's parents but certification can only come from our main office in Kansas which deals with refugees who were granted asylum after 9/11."

"So, can't the Kansas office just email the certification to you?"

"They don't have email."

"Right. So you'll have them fax it, that works!"

"They can't fax."

"Right. And why, exactly, can't they fax?"

"We have to see the original government seal. It's in the regulations."

"Right." My pep is waning. For the love of God...his parents are twenty minutes over the border...can't he just go home? "And even though the Office of Refugee Status has told you by phone that Wani *does indeed* have legal asylum in the States and

39

the papers are coming by mail, he's still can't go home to his parents?"

"I'm afraid not."

"And there's no exception to the regulation, just based on common sense?

"Never," Officer Ramirez replies.

"Alrighty, then."

Wani pipes up, "So do we get to eat lunch now?"

"Well, that's up to the officer," I say, trying guilt. "Oh, he can eat lunch, as long as it's in Mexico. That kid isn't crossing the border."

Shit. Let's review: we've got Wani, a hungry eleven-year-old Sudanese refugee wearing a Fox Studios ID badge with a picture of a 19th-century naval frigate on it, who is separated from his loving family who have sought asylum from their war-torn country and me, adorned with a matching boat ID tag, apparently, a child smuggler and starver of children.

Officer Ramirez considers Wani, then walks to her desk, makes a phone call of ridiculous length, opens her lunch sack and returns with a bag of Lays potato chips and a tangerine which Wani gratefully accepts.

" OK," she starts. "Here's how we're going to do this. I got an exception to the…"

"Fabulous!" I interrupt.

"…paperwork issue," she finishes. "Here's the deal. You've got one exit visa to take the boy back to the United States and reunite with his family."

"That's great!" I say. "And then we'll need another visa for next week for a matching shot the director has to have." Wani stands directly behind Russell, camera left. Officer Ramirez's eyes narrow.

"I don't know what those words mean," she says. "You're not listening."

I stand straighter. My better listening posture. "One visa. One time. It's an exit visa, as in 'go away and don't come back.'"

"Riiiight," I say, slowly, my eyes glazing over. "OK. The one teensy problem with that is we need him back on Tuesday to match a shot we've already got in the can. You see, Wani stands directly behind Russell Crowe, clearly on camera. We have to match it. Wani is absolutely necessary for the continuity of the shot."

Officer Ramirez doesn't mull this over very long. "Are you kidding me? Russell Crowe? What's he done since *Gladiator*? This child needs to be home with his family and back in school with his classmates." Then, leaning down to Wani, she says, "I bet you're in fourth grade, aren't you, son?"

"*Uh,* huh," Wani replies, peeling the tangerine. "Mrs. Bernstein's class. She plays the accordion." Officer Ramirez stares directly at me implying this proves her point. Which is, apparently, that the boy needs to get an education, including music appreciation, and should not be separated from his family, in order to work on a movie, with Russell Crowe, no less, in a foreign country.

At this point, I switch to pleading. "But we have his father's written permission and a child labor permit and he's well taken care of at the studio, schooled on location, and he gets great food."

"Really good food." Wani nods, wolfing chips.

Officer Ramirez shifts her weight, and folds her arms over her uniformed chest. "One visa. One date. You choose." Shit. OK. Shit. Shit. Shit.

"Could we have just a quick minute here? I need to huddle

41

with Wani."

"Oh, no problem, Miss. She nods toward the clock. The US Border Patrol is at your disposal."

I make my face pretend a smile.

"Now, can we go to catering?" Wani asks.

"I'm trying to pull that off, sweetheart. Hang on."

Wani's father, Mr. Chol, escaped, barely, with his family from the Sudanese genocide in 1999. Father of five, he bags groceries at Ralph's Supermarket earning $12.20 per hour. His wife takes in ironing and cares for their four children in their two-bedroom rented, run-down house.

I get Mr. Chol on the phone and explain the situation to him.

Silence, then, "That is a lot of fuss about one boy standing."

"I know," I say, deciding agreement is the way to go here.

"His mother and I expected him home today so he could come with us to church on Sunday. Church is the most important for family. And Monday he has school."

"Right," I say.

"But let me remind you that Wani also goes to school at the studio. And there are plenty of churches in Rosarito so I could take him this Sunday if you'd like." And then toss in. "And did I mention that Wani is paid even for the weekend, when he's not filming?"

Then Mr. Chol asks, "What does Wani want to do?"

I lean down to Wani and ask, "Your father wants to know, what do you want to do?"

"I want a bicycle."

"Excuse me?"

"I want a bicycle. The blue one. For $229.00. So I need $101.00 more from the movie."

"How much do you have now?" I ask, loving where this

42

conversation is going.

"$28.00."

Doing quick math, I add up the days Wani has already worked on set. "You should have over $500.00 by now, Wani. Did you get all your checks?"

"I gave them to my father for food and to turn the lights back on. I got to keep $100.00. I bought some Nikes and chimichangas at Taco Bell for me and my brother. Now I have $28.00."

"Gotcha." Too bad the Nikes weren't on sale. *Don't pay retail,* I think. Then, "You're sure you want to go back to work at the studio? Cause I can take you home right now if you want to go. And whatever you decide is fine with me."

"If I go home right now can I come back and finish filming next week?"

"I'm afraid not, sweetheart."

Who will be the serving boy standing behind Mr. Captain?

Good point. I didn't have that part figured out yet. Clearly, I'd need to find a photo double, a small, sweet-faced, blue-black-skinned, four-foot-tall, amazing African boy, with a valid green card. What the hell, I had two days to pull off that feat.

"You don't need to worry about that, Wani. I only want you to do what you want to do," I lie. "Nothing else is important." This was total bullshit on my part.

"I want the blue bicycle." And it was settled.

With my second phone call, explaining Wani's wishes, Mr. Chol was satisfied that I would care for his son and would drive him over the border and deliver him home on Wednesday.

"Providing no re-shoots are necessary," I hasten to add.

"I trust you to return my son to me on Wednesday, Mrs. Judy." On that day, he is finished with the movie, he returns to his family and goes back to school. "Respectfully, do you

43

understand?"

"Yes, sir."

"Thank you. And please, he must continue to call home everyday."

"Absolutely, Mr. Chol. And thank you for your patience and understanding."

"You are most welcome. I expect him at church on Sunday."

"Absolutely." And when I hang up, though I'm a Buddhist, I make the sign of the cross: up, down, left, right...kind of a knee-jerk warm-up for Sunday.

"What did my father say?" asks Wani.

"Your father said we should turn the car around and get you back to the studio for movie lunch," I improvise. "He also said I'm to take you to church on Sunday and home for good on Wednesday."

"Is that enough days to buy the blue bike?"

"It definitely is, with money left over for chimichangas at Taco Bell!"

"I have to go to church?"

"We both have to go to church. No exceptions. We'll go for chicken mole after."

I plant Wani back in front of George Bush again and dial the production office in Rosarito as it's dawned on me I should apprise our film producer so I'm not the only person on the payroll aware of the Wani situation.

The producer, Duncan Henderson who is wicked smart, experienced, and not without a sense of humor, listens without interruption to my entire saga and then says, "Let me get this straight. You are attempting to smuggle an eleven-year-old African refugee, who lacks proper legal documentation across the border claiming Fox Studios needs him for our movie and in

44

the process of smuggling that child back across the border into the United States he is currently detained at US Border Patrol by a woman with a gun. Is that correct?"

"Um…technically yes. That's one way to explain it," I reply.

"Is it accurate?"

"Well, yes," I say meekly. "But they all have guns, not just the woman." Attempting humor to defuse.

"OK, more guns. That's not cheering me up. Have you made contact with his family? Do his parents know he's safe?"

"Of course, I'm not a total idiot!" I say.

"I beg to differ," Duncan replies. Silence. I'm not about to make a move. And then he says, "OK, is the kid shot out?"

"Not exactly. There's a matching shot on the advance on the call sheet scheduled for next Tuesday, interior Captain's Cabin, Scene seventeen."

"And where is the boy in that scene?"

Shit. I make the sign of the cross again and this time put my fingers to my lips at the end, just like Sean Connery did when he played that monk in. *The Name of the Rose*. And then I say, "Directly behind Russell."

Here let me stop the hemorrhaging and cut to the montage…

The producer instructs me to get myself, the child and Fox Studio out of this. "Grave and potentially very embarrassing situation…Right. Now."

He announces that I will drive Wani over the border to his parents as soon as scene seventeen is shot, *but not before* we get the report from the lab that the film is not damaged. And then he hangs up.

We get the visa. Wani gets a package of HoHos from Officer Ramirez.

45

Officer Ramirez escorts us out of the Border Patrol Office and into the heat from hell in that four p.m. Tijuana August. She extends her hand to shake mine, saying, "I'm just doing the job I was hired to do. Keeping the borders to America safe from terrorism."

I glance at Wani, the potential terrorist, who is still eleven, has melted chocolate and flecks of HoHo cake on his bottom lip, left cheek, and most of his ID badge. Then I look up at Officer Ramirez and decide, for once in my life, to keep my mouth shut. I really need to get the hell out of here with the kid.

"Well, once again, thank you for the visa and the HoHos. And if there's nothing else, we'll say goodbye and head back to the studio."

"There is one more thing, actually," she says.

For the love of God, I'm thinking…what else? You wanna strip search him? He likes blue bikes, chimichangas, and accordion music. He's not a terrorist, he's a geek. But I say, "Yes, something else?"

Deliberately, Officer Ramirez unbuttons her starched uniform breast pocket, pulls out a picture and hands it to me.

The picture shows two adorable little girls in matching striped yellow jumpers both wearing pink duck barrettes at the bottom of their long brown pigtails. "They're my twins"— Officer Ramirez beams—"and they tap dance."

Born a Brat

*"I wonder if we military brats aren't most accurately seen
in light of the pursuit of belonging."*
– Mary Edwards Wertsch – Military Brats

How does one train to become a migrant film worker? I was born
into it.

Raised a military brat in an Air Force family, my first
marching orders, at age five, were to give away most of what I
owned as we packed to join our father at Misawa Air Force Base,
a US military facility on Northern Honshu, Japan. Two hundred
and twenty-five miles north of Tokyo, Misawa, in Aomori
prefecture, our district, was known for its snow-filled winters. In
April, rains give way to glorious springs filled with the exquisite
light pink and white Japanese cherry blossoms of sakura trees.

My father, Albert Bouley (pronounced boolay), reported to
the base in Japan six months before we could join him. During
that six months, how my mother singlehandedly raised three kids
under the age of nine, I'll never understand.

The day finally came when my father was informed his
family could join him, and we started packing. The military
allowed only forty-two lbs. of personal belongings per person to
be shipped overseas. My Barbie doll alone, with all her gear,
weighed over a pound! Though only in first grade, I was already
winging my way into my first international adventure. But first,
I had to lose all my stuffed animals and my Dr. Seuss books.

On a snowy February 7, 1961, Dad was on the base tarmac anxiously awaiting the arrival of our family: my mother, Nina; older sister, Sandi, age nine; and younger brother, Mark, age three. I turned six on the airplane ride to Japan! It took a mere twenty-seven hours on MATS aircraft, Military Air Transport Service, which was a propeller-driven C-135; a huge fat-bodied green airplane. My mother, we three kids, and over seventy Air Force soldiers filled the flight from Travis Air Force base to Wake Island to Tokyo. One soldier provided a great service to my mother by holding me on his lap while I episodically and loudly vomited. The co-pilot gave me a pack of gum hoping that would relieve my nausea. No such luck.

Our lunch and dinner meals on the airplane were sloppy joes, mashed potatoes, and green jello. During our four-hour layover at Wake Island, we were served a meal…of sloppy joes, mashed potatoes, and green jello. MATS aircraft was no Singapore Airlines, I assure you.

My father wanted to raise his children in a Japanese culture and opted out of accepting base housing quarters, where we would have been living in a military community full of Americans. Instead, he rented a tiny two-bedroom turquoise blue stucco Japanese house in the 'machi,' the town in Misawa. It was home. The exterior wooden door opened onto a mudroom. One wall, lined with pine shelves, held our shoes and rain boots. My boots, shiny and bright lavender, were definitely needed in the cold northern Honshu climate. The interior door to the house, made of wood and rice paper squares, slid open to reveal beige straw tatami mats covering the living room floor. We had a ridiculously tiny American-style kitchen; minuscule dining nook; two teeny bedrooms, one for Mark (he always got his own room!) and one that Sandi and I shared. My parents slept on a

48

futon, the traditional Japanese bedding made of a padded mattress, placed on the tatami floor and covered themselves with a thick quilted bedcover. Each night, my parents would unroll their futon, sleep in the living room and roll their futon up in the morning.

My favorite feature in the house was the coolest Japanese-style bathroom ever, with a four-foot tile tub and a wooden bucket for dipping water to pour over yourself once you were clean. Standing on the tile floor using the bucket to rinse my lathered self, I loved watching suds and water drain away in the concave middle of the room. The bathroom was my favorite room in the house specifically because it was different than what we had in America. Early on, I was drawn to different...people, cultures, languages, and bathrooms.

I loved Japan. All of it: the kindness of the Japanese people, who adored children, the food...especially sushi, pickled ginger, and purple Kyoho grapes, all of which I ate with chopsticks. I loved my sweet Japanese friends. I watched them walk to school on rainy days in their yellow slickers. I loved the festivals, particularly the Bon Odori festival. Performed on the fifteenth of August, the festival is a Japanese Buddhist custom to honor the spirits of one's ancestors. My cotton kimono, adorned in flowers the colors of rose, mint, and lemon made me feel pretty and special. On a raised wooden tower in the middle of the circle of dancers, a musician slapped a steady rhythm on a huge hollow taiko drum. Sandi and I danced to that beat. On our feet, we wore traditional Japanese footwear—white cotton socks called tabi, and geta, a wooden combination of clogs and flip-flops. The getas elevated base made my petite frame grow two inches.

I especially loved speaking Japanese—the feel of staccato syllables forming in my mouth. My accent was good. I was often

49

complimented on my pronunciation and the physical form my body would take, with a slight bow of humility as I said, "*Ohayo gozaimasu*" (good morning) or "*Watashi no Nihon-mei wa Junkodesu*" (my Japanese name is Junko). Of the three Bouley children, I was the one who most took to the culture of our adopted home. I prayed we would be able to live forever in Japan. I felt more Japanese than I did American.

As I grew up, I loved playing with words. If I could turn the clock back, I would become an ardent student of languages. A translator. A professor at the Sorbonne.

I craved Japanese food. Soba was, and still is, one of my favorites. 'Briiiing,' the bell on the bike of a young Japanese girl would sound, and our entire family began salivating. 'Briiing,' the bell sounded again as she reached our house. The next sound was our rice paper door sliding open—the young girl, probably fifteen, delivering four bowls of ramen soba, thick noodles in a rich miso broth, with scallions and one piece of pink and white fish cake floating on top in each bowl. Delicious! The cost at that time was 356 yen ($1.00) for four bowls of soba which fed the five of us. When we were finished, we'd slide open our front door, place the used bowls in the mudroom, and shortly after that, the bowls would be picked up by the girl, ringing her bell to thank us as she pedaled down the road.

Most Friday nights, when my father came home from the flight line, where he was crew chief responsible for the maintenance and safety of the C-47s, we would go to the machi to our favorite barayaki restaurant where my father would cook fresh steak and onions with shoju (soy sauce) on a hibachi (hot grill) at our table. It was a blast!

"Kids, make sure you go to the bathroom before we leave," Mom would say. "You know I don't want you using the

50

bathroom in the restaurant." The 'bathroom' was a hole in the ground flanked by two small pieces of wood where we put our feet while we squatted over the hole and 'bombs away.' It was fantastic! Obediently, all three of us kids would pee before we left home. Then we'd jam into our family car, a powder blue Volkswagen Beetle, and off we went on the short ride to the barayaki restaurant.

"Irasshaimase..." This was the greeting of the older woman, the obasan, who met us at the door. The literal translation is: "Welcome."

"Irasshaimase!" the greeting rang out from the kitchen by her ottoson (husband). The sharp, delicious smell of freshly grilled onions and the tsssss noise of thinly sliced beef hitting the hot hibachi griddle made a delicious symphony of scent and sound.

The small wooden restaurant had packed dirt floors, a black potbellied stove, and the piece de resistance—a television! As soon as we arrived, the obasan would change the channel on the TV. Off went the judo match and on came Highway Patrol or Bonanza, or a Felix the Cat cartoon. All in Japanese! When we finally returned to the states, I was stunned that Americans watched these shows too! But they watched in English...clearly not as exotic as watching in Japanese, with no subtitles. To this day, I can sing the Japanese version of the Felix the Cat overture!

"Mom, I have to go to the bathroom. Really. I really have to go. Emergency this time!"

Mom gave me the look then sighed. "Take her to the bathroom please, Sandi, and make sure she washes her hands. And hurry, your dinner will get cold."

Sandi sighed. "I always have to watch her."

"Watch your tone of voice, young lady," my father said. "Do

as your mother says. Take your sister. Don't let her fall in." We scurried off to the banjo (bathroom) accessible only through the kitchen. Chopping scallions and fresh ginger, obasan and ottosan laughed and handed us sugar treats as we waltzed past them to the hole in the ground. Our barayaki dinners were precious times for our family.

To their credit, my parents were great at immersing us in different cultures, specifically in Japan where my father was stationed from 1960–1964. It was the greatest four years of my childhood. I absorbed the culture and customs through Judo, Ikebana (the art of flower arranging), Japanese dance, festivals, and the amazing food.

My sister and I attended geisha school on a sporadic basis. Mom had made arrangements with the owner of the local geisha school to teach her son, Kazuo, American customs as he was planning to go to the states to become a surgeon. In return, my sister and I were invited to the school to study Japanese customs: how to tie an obi, learn traditional songs and dances, the rudiments of the tea ceremony.

Japan was home. I loved it. Then 1964 arrived and with it, our return to America. Not my favorite chapter.

We had other food traditions. By order of Colonel Cat, our base commander, a blue canvas duffel bag was kept by our front door. The bag, issued to every family, was filled with C rations, our emergency food if we needed to evacuate to a bunker, raid shelter, should we be under attack, or while the Russians practiced their war exercises. The rations were packaged in unappetizing dark green tin cans. There was a cool, tiny can opener (as opposed to a regular, boring, civilian can opener) that was fun to use. Remember, I was six. The contents inside the bag included: boned canned chicken, pretend meat stew, crackers (stale), peanut butter (dry), powdered milk (stupid) and my personal favorite: Good 'n' Plentys: black licorice candy coated with hardened sugar dyed pink and white. I polished those off in no time.

One day my mother asked, "OK. Which one of you ate all the Good 'n' Plentys?"

Sandi and Mark said, "I didn't." I stalled, in case they changed their mind and confessed out of kindness to protect me. No such luck. So finally, I raised my hand, guilty, embarrassed and wondering what my punishment would be. Turned out to be no dessert for one week. In retrospect, the punishment fit the crime. Punishment was typical in our family. Sometimes we got restriction, sometimes the leather strap on our bare bottoms. Should that have happened today, Child Protective Services would intervene. But this was the early '60s. Spare the rod, spoil the child. Our military father believed in corporal punishment, even if you were six.

The duffel bag contained enough food for a week if we needed to subsist that long in the bunker. Periodically, for training purposes, a piercing siren would sound which meant my father or mother would round up our family, grab the duffel bag and scurry us off to the air raid shelter. At school, we had air raid drills. As soon as the screech alert sounded, every kid in school and their teachers dashed under their desks and stayed there until the all-clear bell rang.

An exercise in escape.

Thinking about that 'normal' act of grabbing our rations bag and going to the air raid shelter on any given school day is similar to making a movie. Be prepared for anything to happen. Have plan B. And C. Don't flinch. Grab a snack.

Brats live a fluid, nomadic, marginal, Bedouin life. In our

family, we submitted to rules. Most importantly, at my mother's instructions, we kept our family's secrets and lies. Plenty of them. My parents' arguments. My father's binge drinking and corporal punishments.

As I grew older, I learned to find some shelter from the storm of my father's episodic anger by providing comic relief with my self-deprecating humor. I could cut through my father's silent treatments by hamming it up, telling funny stories about things that happened at school.

I was a do-er of things. I took ballet (hated it), practiced judo (loved it!) Got great grades and was voted 'personality plus,' for which I received a plaque. My mother beamed and said, to anyone who would listen, "That's my daughter!" It didn't dawn on me until I was an adult that her narcissism and codependency would be the chasm in our relationship. She wanted to be my best friend. What I needed was a mother.

No matter where we were stationed, on the first day of school Mom reminded us, "Don't get too close to your new friends because either their fathers or your dad will likely be transferred to their next assignment. You'll just have to say goodbye. It's better not to get close than to be broken-hearted." Through most of my adult life, I continued to carry out my mother's questionable instructions. This contributed in part to my unsteady love relationships in which I had one foot in, one foot out. 'Nice to meet you, where's the exit?' My father taught me to always keep my passport current and never own any more than I could pack in an afternoon.

Our family crest was 'temporary.'

Once I disobeyed my mother's instructions about not getting close to friends but instead, be prepared to leave them or have them leave me. My one exception was Hitomi Wannamaker.

Petite and pretty, Hitomi had all the best features from her Caucasian American father and her beautiful Japanese mother. Hitomi and I were best friends for two years before her father was transferred. We had sleepovers at each other's quarters (they weren't called homes) where we played the board game, Barbie, Queen of the Prom. Usually, Hitomi's dad got pizza for us. One winter we helped my father make an igloo in our backyard. Hitomi and I promised to be friends forever. We hoped that our fathers would end up assigned to the same base in the future. Alas, Hitomi's father transferred out. As it turned out, our correspondence lasted only a short time. No Facebook in those days, no cell phone texting. Just letter writing which we did and phone calls which we didn't do because international calls were too expensive. Our fathers were never stationed together again. We soldiered on and met the next batch of Air Force Brats.

Raised in a transient life, I often feel I'm on the outside looking in, wondering how to belong. Lacking roots, my understanding of the verb 'to be' is incomplete. The one question I could never answer on an English exam: define permanence (um…when you don't have to go to the air raid shelter?) Some things will muck me up. For example, setting up online accounts to pay bills. I hated answering the security questions: What is the name of your first school?

My answer: I don't know.

What is the name of the first street you lived on?

My answer: No idea.

What is the name of your third-grade school teacher?

My answer: Are you high? I don't even know the name of the school.

I've met plenty of other Brats in film. We quickly recognize and welcome each other. We're used to fitting in and making temporary friends, that's the easy part. The hard part is staying. Can't find home here…move on—to the next place or the next relationship. Move on to the next movie. The key is to keep moving.

The skills transfer well if you're stuck making a movie with folks you can't stomach. Producer an ass? Not to worry, you wrap in five months and never have to see him again.

Remember your Brat creed—take a temporary approach to the world… "I'm doing this for now." If the movie is stupid (and occasionally they are) just get through it, get your check, your wrap gift, your credit and get on a plane.

My passport with all its brightly colored stamps is my badge of honor. Finding my true self underneath the chameleon continues to be my scavenger hunt.

The truth is, I'm still searching for where I'm from. I hope it's wherever I'm going next.

In the Beginning – How I Joined the Circus

Peter O'Toole HATES the color brown!
– Judith Bouley, Author

How the hell did I get into show business? I was working for Child Protective Services as a social worker, got laid off, rehired at a higher salary (go figure) as a supervisor in CPS with the responsibility of creating statistical charts and graphs tracking how many children in our county were molested, abused, abandoned, or neglected. Instead of actually saving the kids! From nine to five, I sat in an office listing numbers and crimes. Repeatedly. X # of boys malnourished, X # of boys sodomized, X # of boys sodomized by multiple perpetrators. Then on to the girls: malnourished, beaten, or impregnated by their uncles. I made pie charts and put checks in neat columns.

I was miserable.

In my short tenure as a social worker, I had worked throughout my community actually saving some kids' lives. I was good at it. Armed with a green, county-issued Pinto, I drove each day to the scene of the crime, any junior high school or church, the uncle's house, a preschool. I was fueled by a bit of courage and a sense of noble purpose.

Sitting at my desk at work one afternoon, I looked up from the report I was writing and, in a completely unpremeditated moment, turned to one of my office mates and said, "Were you ever molested?"

The older woman who sat across from me quickly said, "Yes. Actually, I was, but I don't remember much about it."

"Were you?" I said to the woman on my right.

Without looking up, she nodded and said, "Yup. Twice."

The child protection services unit CPS was made up of seven women and one man.

I polled the room to discover six of the seven women, including me, had suffered some sort of child abuse. Four of the six of us were survivors of sexual abuse.

Specifically because of our own traumatic experiences, we were women who could listen, look into the face of a wounded child, and say with honesty, "I understand. I'm here to protect you." I believe there are times when it is possible to heal our own wounds by helping others.

In 1984, Reagan was czar, and Proposition thirteen had passed with the mental health clinic doors open, and tens of thousands of pathetically sick souls were pushed out onto the street. At CPS, six of us were laid off. I was last hired and first fired. One month later, I was rehired as a supervisor drowning in paperwork.

So there I was, with my charts and graphs. No longer helping others.

Arriving home from work each evening, I made the same pronouncement: "I *really* can't do this anymore. I'm dying on the vine here."

My boyfriend at the time, John: handsome, charming, and completely unemployed said, "Quit."

"Yeah. Right," I replied.

"You hate this job. The way I see it, Judy, the only other thing you need to write at work is a one-line memo: 'Dear supervisor, this is a stupid job. I quit.'"

The following day, I did the math on how much I could earn with unemployment benefits, tips from a waitressing job, and $10.00 per hour teaching jazzercise four nights a week. Just enough to support my boyfriend, his son, and me. How's *that* for codependency?

The next day, I turned in my five-line memo which read:

"Dear Supervisor,

Social Work is the most honorable thing I've done in my life. Statistical analysis isn't.

I no longer wish to be employed in my current job with the county. I am giving you my two weeks' notice beginning today.

Please know that if a social worker position in CPS becomes available I'd take it in a heartbeat and be forever grateful. I thank you for all I've learned under your supervision and hope you understand my need to follow my heart."

With all respect,

Judy

My supervisor called me into her office at the end of the day and said, "This is the best memo I've ever received on county stationary."

Two weeks later, on my last day at work, she took me to lunch. She promised to call when a social worker position became available. Then she hugged me and said, "But I have a feeling you're going to go on to bigger and better things. Who knew I would, in short order, call Tom Hanks my co-worker (Turner and Hooch, with the slobbery dog. We had a machine that manufactured slob when Hooch ran dry.)

Before the unemployed boyfriend became that, he had a full,

creative career in the film business in Hollywood, in the '70s, when films like *Days of Heaven*. As his son was heading toward his dreadful teenage years, the boyfriend decided it was time to get him out of Los Angeles and into a healthier lifestyle. They moved to Santa Cruz, where we met one late afternoon at a popular fish joint on the wharf, where I worked as a waitress. This was 1979. I had tested for the job at CPS and had a three-month waiting period before I was hired. My sister worked at the restaurant and hired me. I was quite bad at the job. "Here you go, sir, one coffee. Oh…hang on, let me get you a spoon." The first day I sliced lemons and bread I needed seven Band-Aids.

John settled onto the stool at the counter with Ian next to him. He ordered two chowders and changed my life. At his suggestion, we volunteered to serve on the local film board in our small, northern California seaside community.

One day in late winter, the phone rang. Peter O'Toole was coming to Santa Cruz to star in the film, *Creator*. In short order, I was hired to help the Casting Director. We arranged an open casting call and processed over eight hundred hopefuls. We hired most. And for my good work, I was paid seventy-five dollars a day and got to wear a walkie-talkie. I was hooked!

Egos were everywhere. Here is the memo we received before Mr. O'Toole arrived:

O'Toole preferences while working (to be followed):

1. Car: Granada or Ford Fairmont (NOT BROWN) four-door.
2. Hotel: Nothing higher than the 5th floor. Mr. O'Toole gets a one-bedroom suite. Kenny gets a single room on the same floor but down the hall from one another.

3. Travel: VIP treatment always! Travel representative and a representative from whatever airline he is flying are to meet him at the airport.

4. Airline seat: First class always! Smoking section.

5. In trailer: A fan. A large supply of sugarless gum (various flavors, NO bubblegum), an icebox filled with: Perrier (he drinks six of the large screw-top per day), a selection of cold cuts and cheese (no fruit), a small bar for entertaining guests, filled with scotch, brandy, vodka, gin, and beer.

6. Schedule: eight a.m. make-up begins. Mr. O'Toole prefers to shoot mid-day to seven p.m.

7. You will rent a house for him no more than fifteen minutes to set. Unfurnished. Rent from Sept 10 to December 31. He receives a refund if he vacates early. You will pay for the house. He will get the refund. Two separate bedrooms. Mr. O'Toole sleeps upstairs, Kenny downstairs. Mr. O'Toole's area should have a large sitting room, den, and large bedroom. They will have two separate phones with unlisted phone #s.

You will reach Kenny on his. Do NOT call Mr. O'Toole!

8. Crucial note: Keep Mr. O'Toole does **not** like the color BROWN!

Seriously? I *swear* the above is true.

Film School

"Jude...just get it the way you want it."
– Dick Broder, my partner

In 1984, I met the man who changed my life forever. With a pork pie hat mashed onto his head of wiry hair, squinty eyes behind aviator-shaped glasses, he was protectively hunched over a small spiral notebook into which he wrote with intense concentration. Every few seconds, he'd give a furtive glance to the left and then right, scanning the perimeter. This guy was barbed wire guarded. At first glance, I assumed Dick Broder was a dope dealer.

He smoked more than he breathed.

We met in Santa Cruz, California on the set of a small independent film titled *Hard Traveling,* which I called 'Rough Going,' because it was. Dick was working as a background actor (also called an extra) in a courtroom scene for $20.00 a day. That came about at the pleading of the script supervisor, Ellen, who was dear friends with Dick. *"Jude, just hire him, please."*

"Why? Something is fishy here. It makes no sense that a man as accomplished as you say he is, with a successful Hollywood career wants to work as a background actor. What gives? There's something else going on here that you're not telling me."

Ellen stared at me for a few seconds, then. "For his personal reasons, which he doesn't want to share, I just can't tell you, Jude, but trust me on this...he needs this job."

"Is he a felon? Did he rob a liquor store, Ellen?"

"I'd cast him as a dope dealer."

"No!" she replied. "He's a great guy and a dear friend. Just do this as a favor for me, Jude. Dick won't let you down."

I trusted Ellen. I was also curious as hell as to what this guy's story was, so I hired him.

I was doing the job of three people on the film: casting, props, and catering at the whopping rate of $250.00 a week...essentially slave wages in the film business, even in 1984. *Hard Traveling* was a great crash course in what 'not to do' in filmmaking. Things on set were a chaotic mess. The assistant director was not pushing the director to stay on schedule. The director, being the director, wanted things his way. No one communicated well (or at all) with the department heads.

The producer was in over her head. In a word...*messy*.

Finally, the producer recognized that they were falling behind schedule which meant the investors' money wouldn't last through the wrap of the movie. Dick mentioned that he had assistant directed and produced in the past. The producer and director decided to try him out for one day as assistant director. Things shaped up on set, immediately. Dick, now the assistant director. He quickly righted the ship. We finished the film...on time. I watched Dick as he worked well with the director, actors, and crew. He watched me being respectful and kind to the actors and background actors.

The Dick and Judy fan club had begun.

Cut to: Three weeks later. My phone rings.

"Hi, Judy. It's Dick Broder. How are you?"

"Fine," I said, because I always do...whether I'm fine or not. *"How about you?"*

"All good on my end. Listen, I'm calling to invite you to lunch if you're available this week. I have a business proposal to

discuss with you."

"*Really?"* I said, intrigued. *"I'll need to ask my boyfriend, John, if it's OK. As a rule, he's not too keen on my dining with other men, even professionally."*

Silence. *"OK. If it's a go, let me know what date works and of course, bring him with you."*

I met boyfriend John in 1979, at a fish diner on the Santa Cruz wharf a few weeks after he and his young son, Ian, arrived in town having just moved from Hollywood, where John was well employed in the film industry. I was a waitress at the diner called Cardinale's. It was likely a front for laundering drug money. Really.

I was dressed in small clothes—a blue crocheted bikini top and cut-offs, sitting at the counter eating clam chowder. Though there was plenty of counter space available, John sat right next to me, his young son to his right. Tousled silver hair, steel blue eyes, and lips created for kissing, John wasted no time chatting me up. "Ian and I just pulled into town today and decided we needed fish and chips before unpacking."

"You came to the right place," I said. "The food is great. I work here. In fact, the food is so good I'm here on my day off!"

"What days do you work?" he asked.

"Monday through Friday, day shift and Saturday night."

"That's a lot of shifts. When do you have time to play?"

I laughed and moved on. "I take as many shifts as I can…stashing money while I'm waiting to be hired by the county as a social worker in the Child Protection department. I tested eight months ago and did well so, in theory, I could be hired any day. I'll miss working here though. It's a great job. The other waitresses are sweethearts. Our customers tell us we're all cute and sassy. I'm actually a shit waitress, forget the spoon when I

64

bring the chowder, but I'm friendly and funny and do pretty well in tips."

He grinned and slowly nodded. "I'll bet you do."

"What about you guys? What brings you to Santa Cruz?"

"It was time to get my son out of the rat race of LA."

John went on to tell me that he about his long, successful career in the entertainment business.

His resume included working as a studio cameraman on The Johnny Carson Show and Laugh-In, working in production on independent feature films and finally working for George Lucas at Industrial Light and Magic in Los Angeles. Because he was well trusted, John's last assignment for George Lucas was to drive the iconic Star Wars' robots, R2D2 and C3PO to ILM's new home in San Anselmo! John said, "I should have held them hostage and gotten some ransom $!"

That should have tipped me off. But I was smitten!

Young son was restless. "Dad, can we go now? We need to get the key to the cabin so we can move in. I wanna unpack." John's cousin, a professor at UCSC owned a small, beautiful cottage in the redwoods of the Santa Cruz hills and had invited John and Ian to stay indefinitely.

John sighed and said, "Ian's right. He always is. We better get going. I'd love to take you to dinner sometime soon, Judy. Let me take your number."

We went to dinner. And kissed. Delicious. More dinners which he cooked for his son and me in their cozy hilltop cabin with a view of the Monterey Bay.

At the time, I was living at my sister, Sandi's house I was sleeping on her couch, helping care for my niece and nephew. One afternoon, two months after our first date, John called and announced, "Let's pack you up. You're living with me now." I packed. Two hours later, he arrived and filled the trunk of his BMW with my belongings.

We loved in love and crazy great sex for two years until I discovered John was dealing cocaine! He was an alcoholic. I tried to 'love' him out of it. I'd throw tantrums. We'd have shitty make-up sex.

Early one Saturday morning, I asked John to sit at our kitchen table. Hung over from the previous night, he lit up a Camel and asked me what was on my mind. "Make a choice, John, me or stay addicted. If you choose to stay with me, you must go to rehab. Full stop."

John looked at me and said, "You are the most amazing woman I have ever known. This is a rugged decision I have to make. I know I am making the worst mistake of my life." And with that John opened the refrigerator, pulled out a Heineken and sat back down. "We can work this out baby. You've been mad at me plenty and you've never left. You're not leaving me now. I truly can't live without you. I refuse to live without you. You won't leave me and you won't leave Ian. You are the only real mother he's ever had. So think hard before you give me empty threats." John finished his beer and, before breakfast, opened another.

"That's it John. I'm packing and leaving today. I'll stay with my sister until I can get my own place. This is a clean break. You won't know where I live or which film I'm on. I'm packing now."

"Who gets Moby?"

"I do!" I said. "Moby has been my dog for a dozen years. Are you crazy?"

"So you are willing to take Moby away from Ian? Moby is the only animal Ian has had."

"This conversation just ended. Enjoy your beer. Correction:

66

your beers. Plural. I will tell Ian. Now." And off I went.

Four hours later, I backed my fully backed yellow Volkswagen down the driveway. Moby sat on my lap, his small head out the window. I took only my clothes, guitar, artwork, and a few books. I left my furniture and all that I had purchased for our home. I left Ian. Sobbing, I didn't look in the rearview mirror. I drove to freedom.

John and I met Dick in a restaurant in Carmel. Since he knew he was the boss of me, Dick spoke mostly to John. He explained his idea of starting an 'umbrella company' with his good friend Ellen Winchell and me providing crew, equipment, and casting for film, television, and commercial productions shooting in the local area. Central Coast Production Services would serve Monterey, Carmel, Big Sur, Santa Cruz, and the smaller surrounding communities. Productions could save thousands of dollars by hiring local crew, instead of importing their shooting crews, which meant expenses for their hotel and per diem. John agreed it was a smart idea, a well-needed company, as nothing like this existed in the Monterey Bay area. Half-way into lunch, John gave Dick and me his blessing, then excused himself to 'go visit a close friend' who owned a jewelry shop nearby. I knew the close friend was one of John's cocaine dealers.

I was gut-stabbed and made excuses to Dick about John's behavior.

My codependency had arrived before my cappuccino.

"I'm sorry about John," I said. *When am I ever going to finally leave him,* I thought.

"Do you want dessert?" Dick replied.

"I'll have crème brûlée," I announced. "It rhymes with my name."

Dick ordered and said, "Any thoughts on what I've

proposed?"

Sassy, I said, "Dessert or creating the company?" Dick drank his coffee. "I'm thrilled to death you believe in me," I said. Since I didn't. "I'm definitely in."

What I didn't know at that time was that Dick was recently out of a halfway house for drug and alcohol addiction. His commitment to the twelve-step program of Alcoholics Anonymous was saving his life, one day at a time. The new company he was creating gave him a way back into his productive life.

We raised sixty thousand dollars in seed money from family and friends, rented an office in Monterey, bought computers and lamps, and opened Central Coast Production Services in 1984.

Within the first six weeks, we had booked thirteen episodes of a series for the Christian Broadcasting Network called *Doris Day's Best Friends*, which included her beige Standard Poodle and Rock Hudson. We shot their iconic 'split-screen' scenes with the two amazing actors.

First project, we hit it out of the park! CBN became returning customers.

Dick and I were well on our way. Each of us brought different strengths to the table.

Dick worked as an assistant director, location manager, and producer. I cast and occasionally managed locations. CCPS was film school for me, Dick was my mentor.

We were successful from the start, employing local film crew, actors, and extras. Rapidly our resumes grew. Consistently, Dick worked in stunning locations nationwide, shooting tons of car commercials for world-renowned advertising agencies; Saatchi and Saatchi, Chiat/Day, Leo Burnett, and most of the others. Dick and the ridiculously talented director, Dusty Nelson,

68

(who *painted with film*), would hang off of camera cars, speeding around corners and down hills at sunrise and sunset.

My natural talent was casting. I loved exploring actors' details, their nuance and specific, unique voices. I prided myself on finding just the right people to breathe into their characters.

Repeatedly, I was hired to work on feature films and some episodic television. The fascinating world of feature casting nabbed me. My first studio feature was shot in Santa Cruz. My assignment was to cast 2,200 background actors and five speaking roles for *The Lost Boys,* a Joel Schumacher film. It was a huge and crazy assignment to cut my teeth on. Following that, *Star Trek IV* found the director and star, Leonard Nimoy, an animatronic whale and me filming at the Monterey Bay Aquarium.

For the major film studios: *Disney, DreamWorks, Warner Bros,* and most of the others, I was hired to work alongside legendary filmmakers, Peter Weir, Robert Zemeckis, Sam Mendes, and a boatload of others, shooting in the US, Argentina, Puerto Rico, Mexico, Bulgaria, Morocco, and India. I won the lottery.

Due to our work schedules, Dick and I were often separated by continents and seasons, but we always shared a checkbook, a partnership, and a base. Both of us slogged through episodic bouts of depression, from our childhoods, bad habits, a lack of belief in ourselves, some of the things depression is made of, but gratefully, we always had each other. Ours was a relationship of shorthand. We knew each other's dreams and fears. Had we not been business partners, we may have been lovers. We never were. And we were closer for it.

Dick was ten years older than me, and decades wiser. I craved his approval. At times, he made me batshit crazy and I returned the favor. But, without question, we covered each other, and in that lack of questioning, we found home.

With Dick and I working on different locations so much of the time, the phone and email became our lifeline. Some nights our phone conversations would go like this:

Me: *"Where are you?"*
Him: *"I dunno, hang on. Let me check the matches in the ashtray. Apparently I'm in Missoula, Montana, how about you?"*

While I was away for extended periods on film locations, Dick would often fax to me in the mornings one page of his stream of consciousness writing. He called it 'fifty-four lines,' which is exactly what one single-spaced page would hold. It always began: "JB and ended with, 'much love, DB,'" In those fifty-four lines, Dick shared and argued with me. He educated me. He thrashed on and on about love, filmmaking, Hollywood as a cesspool, parenthood, politics, music, and movies. Dick wrote about the weight of a handgun or a broken heart. I loved his fifty-four lines.

Complex, at times twisted in his thinking, Dick always wrote his truth. His favorite saying to me was, "Just get it the way you want it, Jude." Such a simple pronouncement yet at times for me an impossible task.

Sadly, as our business got stronger, my personal life got weaker.

Don't Cry for Me Argentina

Oh What a Circus, Oh What a Show!
— Andrew Lloyd Webber, Tim Rice

In 1996, I worked on an amazing film in Buenos Aires. Directed by the Englishman Alan Parker, we filmed in Buenos Aires. I took the gig because Alan's films had affected me quite viscerally, specifically: *Pink Floyd, The Wall; The Commitments and Midnight Express.*

For *Evita,* I needed to find the perfect actors for thirty-eight roles and from four thousand background actors needed, Alan and I selected the foreground of the background, those working closest to the leads.

Evita is one of the films I'm most proud of. Understating it, the film was a highly rewarding and excruciating experience.

We needed tango dancers. Searching the milongas, the clubs, and the streets of San Telmo and La Boca, I discovered all we needed, including a thin fourteen-year-old dark-haired girl dancing with her working-class father. She was tiny; he was protective. A stubby grandmother, nearing eighty, the thick folds of her bloated feet spilling out of worn stiletto heels, joined out elite group of dancers. At a tango club, watching her dance, her passion so moved me, I cried. She shrugged at my reaction and lit a cigarette. "If I do not dance, I die." She made the cut with an extreme close-up of her feet dancing in a dirty puddle of rain.

Among the many principal roles I cast, I searched at great

71

length for a young girl to play the nine-year-old version of Madonna, who played the star of the film, Eva Peron. Agents sent headshots and resumes of their young talent. I met with my favorites. I met girls through numerous casting calls, met with mothers and daughters who crashed my auditions. I searched everywhere for the child nervous as hell as I kept striking out. The clock was ticking. I was frustrated with my weeks' work of meeting young girls in tutus and petticoats, go-go boots, and tiny tight dresses…all of them curtsying and saying their lines in sing-song voices, no nuance, no feeling, no truth. Mothers assured me that their already stick-thin eight-year-old daughters were dieting for the role! Insanity.

I was nervous, not relishing the idea of telling the director we may need to import the girl from Mexico City. The producers, who guard their budget like the crown jewels, were all over me to cast this important role locally. My next plan: search the local orphanages.

One morning, I was unpacking my backpack in my beautiful casting room replete with a fireplace, in the third-floor conference room I was using for taping auditions. My assistant opened the door and brought in nine-year-old Maria Lujan Hidalgo.

A petite nine years old with a natural sadness in her eyes, Maria shook my hand and sat in the chair across from mine. We talked for a few minutes about her family, school, and her friends, and then I talked with her about the character. The scene involved Maria playing the young Eva Duarte at her father's funeral alongside Madonna, who played the adult Eva Duarte. Maria had no questions for me. She got on her mark, the piece of blue tape I had placed on the floor to accommodate my camera focus, and began. Her lines were delivered perfectly, in agonizing fear and sadness. She draped herself over our makeshift coffin (a small loveseat) and cried like the broken young fatherless child she was. *Hell, yes!* I thought. Alan would love her. I ticked that one off my list. Only thirty-seven more roles to cast.

Some weeks later, Alan told me he needed me to go to Budapest to cast the huge funeral scenes, which needed thousands of extras for the huge funeral scene. I panicked. I simply couldn't do it. I couldn't split myself casting in Argentina and casting in Hungary at the same time. I didn't feel my team in Buenos Aires was strong enough to step into my shoes and didn't believe there was enough time to prep Budapest. I was exhausted. And my Hungarian was a little limp. I told Alan I was sorry, but I couldn't go. He was livid.

I continued casting—Parker wouldn't speak to me. He barred me from going to set. I was not allowed to watch dailies (the film we shot the day before). Simply, Alan trusted me, loved my great work, and needed me in Budapest. As a man who was used to always getting what he wanted, it was unthinkable that I would say no to him, a word he wasn't used to hearing.

For the rest of my time casting Argentina, Alan was brutishly angry.

Meanwhile, back in real life, my grandmother, one of my favorite beings on the planet, was in her home in Santa Cruz, California. In a coma. At age eighty-two with a list of serious ailments, my grandmother made a conscious decision to die, refusing medication, food and water. She was simply done and wanted to move on to whatever was next.

I flew back from Argentina, sat at her bedside, and played Malagueña on the guitar. Over and over. She stirred once or twice at the music and responded when I touched her hand.

The Tibetan Book of the Dead, and basic physics say that

hearing is the last sense to go.

I believe that so I communicated through music and told sweet stories of our past adventures. I told her I was proud of her strength and guts and that I respected her decision. I massaged her hands and feet.

After Nana's death, the family divvied up her stuff. I got her Scrabble game. It was well-worn over our years of use on Friday nights. On Scrabble nights, Nana had one generous shot of Jack Daniels, over two ice cubes, in Baccarat crystal. I drank wine. We made words and recorded scores. We talked about everything...including how our everyone in our family played the word game—on the Scrabble board and in life. We had unspoken rules and stayed silent with our words which should have been shared. We kept score through anger and resentments.

After Nana's death, it dawned on me that suicide is a seven-letter word. Had she simply been playing she'd have gotten an extra fifty points for using all seven of her words. In the end, though other family members disagreed, I knew Nana had won. She was through with this life and wanted to push the forward button. I miss her and always will. I revere her courage.

On February 5, my birthday, the landline in my office in Buenos Aires rang.

Mom: Quietly. *"Happy birthday, honey."*

Me: *"Thanks, Mom. I miss you guys."*

Mom: *"Honey, I'm sorry to tell you, with you so far away. Nana died this morning."*

Me: Silent. Tears. *"Thanks for calling, Mom. I need to go to singing rehearsals now.*

"Madonna will be there and I want to keep an eye on my people."

74

Mom said, *"OK. Take care of yourself, Judy. I love you."*

I echoed her, hung up, and went to singing rehearsals. I couldn't connect with any of my emotions. I couldn't allow myself to be sad. I had work to do. Hundreds of people were counting on me. That was my way out of feeling my feelings. Stay busy. Stay distracted.

"Judy, your services are no longer needed on the film," the producer said. "You've done a great job. Alan and I thank you. And now it's time for you to move on."

What? I thought. "What?" I said. "But we still have three weeks of filming here. I've never left a film early. What's going on?"

"Again, let me say that your job is finished here. Your services are no longer needed. We wish you could have seen your way through to do the casting in Budapest, not just in Buenos Aires. Please turn in your petty cash receipts, sign out with accounting, and pack up. The travel coordinator will sort out your return trip."

I turned in my receipts, went to the Plaza Hotel, where I'd lived for the previous four months, and went straight into the bathroom where I stared at my own reflection and said out loud...

I hate you, Judy. Regardless of circumstances, guilty or not guilty, it was my well-worn practice to make myself wrong. *I hate you, Judy.*

I called Dick. "For the first time in my life, I just got fired. Parker is pissed I won't do the casting in Budapest. I can't. I can't figure out how to be in two places at one time. The window for prep is rapidly closing. Alan is shooting the huge funeral scene there. He'll need thousands of extras. How am I supposed to cast in Budapest while I'm still casting in Buenos Aires? There are casting people in Hungary. What the fuck do I do, Dick?"

75

"Come home, Judy. Life's too short to hang around with assholes. You've done brilliant work. Feel pride. Acknowledge that. Pack. Buy a present for me and come home. You're missed."

Again, Dick's words rescued me. I flew home two days later, after first making certain my assistants knew how to cast what little Parker needed to finish the Buenos Aires portion of the film. Strapped into my seat on the plane, over and over I played the 'getting fired' conversation in my brain. How could I have been so stupid? How could I have let Parker down? Why couldn't I do what I felt was impossible? Why can't I learn to change stupid me and be a better person?

I continued that refrain for one year after I left the film. Simply and sadly, I was my own worst enemy. I shared with Dick my ugly thoughts.

"I don't understand, Jude. You're so uniquely talented. Anyone of these guys are lucky, full stop, to have you work on their films. So many people love and respect you. Why do you think so little of yourself? You have to work that out, Jude. You just gotta get it the way you want it."

Easy enough for him to say. Dick seemed to have gotten it the way he wanted it...happily married, well-respected in the industry, earning great money working on commercials and films. I hoped I could get it the way I wanted it. I tried to will myself to believe it. But always in the back of my mind was that constant question...*what was wrong with me?*

And Then Dick Wrote

There is music here, Jude...and it is jazz.
— Dick Broder, my partner and best friend.

My partner, Dick deserves his own chapter.

Often separated by great distances, sometimes by seasons, Dick and I kept ourselves nourished through our daily routine of fifty-four lines. The fax machine would spit out one single-spaced page. I would devour every word and then re-read. Then I would send my fifty-four pages.

My birthday missive when I turned forty:

"So what have you gone and done? You have a vast resume of personal and professional accomplishments and a host of adoring fans. You come from a place that begins, 'what can I do for you?' Never a bad beginning and one that comes from a pervasive feeling of inclusion and acceptance for those around you no matter their station. This is a rare quality to discover in any environment let alone 'Hollywood!'

"You're a good girl, Judy Bouley, and I count you very high on the list of people I admire. Look at what you've managed to do with the resources that were available: a remarkable career that you just about invented, a wonderful home of your own, a solid record of saving and investing and a generosity displayed toward others. You have an extended family that goes from coast to coast, country to country—many of whom consider you the epicenter and their spiritual leader. You maintain an ever-

77

expanding list of happy clients and loyal assistants all of whom would follow you into any battle anywhere, anytime.

"And standing in the wings, always on the edges and seams, stands your partner of fourteen years, lending a word of encouragement or a well-placed barb, whatever the situation calls for. Let me just say that I have had unprecedented access to your world and I have appreciated the privilege. It has been an education and a constant source of entertainment, frustration, joy, and pride. Much love, DB."

On my 50th birthday:

"Cheer up...fifty isn't that bad. Most people think your life is great. I know I do. You have had an intense decade but have much to show for it. Having a personal life isn't mutually exclusive to having a profession. Stop isolation! You do that whether you're working or not. Therapy has a way of becoming a way of life, so, be careful. Jude. You are close to having it MADE. If you could only entertain the idea that you are capable and deserving of a more fulfilling life it could be yours. You are as pretty as you are smart so let that part of you show. Much love, DB."

And the night before, I stood up for him as his best man at his wedding.

"Yet another road we cross together. I can't imagine crossing it without you standing by my side with your eye on my back, covering me, encouraging me and wanting only the best for me. That, my dear, is irreplaceable in the known universe. Butch Cassidy never had it so good. Laurel and Hardy never managed half the laughs we've had."

"Although, we play in different bands, you in the symphony, me in the combo, we march through life stride for stride never leaving each other too far out of step. There is music here, Jude, and it's jazz. We will never cease riffing together. Never!"

"I love you, adore you and admire your courage, faith, and ability to reverse any adversity, overcome any obstacle and land firmly on your feet with your eyes cast forward. You are unafraid."

"You're my first, last and best partner, friend and fellow traveler. Rock on! Much love, DB."

And I wrote: "I miss you forever, Dick. Much love, JB."

Road to Perdition

It's never the changes we want that changes everything.
    – Junot Diaz

Chicago. Winter. Freezing. It was so bitterly cold I cried. The wind, off the lake made it feel as if ice picks were crammed into my ears. But, when you need to recreate Chicago during the depression, in the dead of winter as a film location, Chicago was a great choice.

Brilliantly directed by the British director, Sam Mendes, the film starred Tom Hanks, Paul Newman, Daniel Craig, and Jennifer Jason Leigh. Jude Law played the creepiest, sinister crime photographer who got off on photographing dead people.

My casting challenge was to populate a city, circa 1930s, with men, women, and children. Sam needed townspeople, cops, Ceili dancers, mafia, nuns, school children, thugs, and a few dead men. Everyone had to be truly Irish.

My great team and I held numerous casting calls which involved tons of advertising, In newspapers, on the radio, with the film commission and through social media. We worked in high school gymnasiums, church meeting rooms, and a few Irish pubs in which I would be hoisted onto the bar, and into a megaphone I announced the needs of our film. Next, the hopefuls completed applications and my staff photographed them. "OK, kids. Thanks so much. Don't call us, we'll call you." A bourbon, neat, appeared for me and then it was time for a game of darts.

The lads wouldn't allow me to leave until I'd shown my skill, which was dreadful. Not quite the typical Hollywood variety casting call.

Though I was far away from my company, Central Coast Production Services, I was still involved as a principal partner. Sadly, our business has taken a turn for the worse. With my partner Dick and I having trained so many film crew, many of them had gone on to work as independent contractors instead of under the auspices of Central Coast. Brilliant as Dick was, his phone stopped ringing. Occasionally, he would work in the Pacific Northwest with his well-established clients. I suspected Dick was having financial challenges as he was the bread winner in their family. I resented Dick's wife, Karen for not working, not contributing financially to their household, especially as Dick's great work was used less and less.

Emails arrived from DB about being depressed. He was devastated that his work was drying up. He didn't understand why he was no longer getting the calls for commercials.

I sent back quick responses and got back to my mountain of work. *"Hang in there, Dick, things always turn around. You know that. Or maybe Karen can help out."*

I said knowing full well she wouldn't. I realize now I should have been more loving, communicated more.

On a movie, my tunnel vision takes over. I am much less in touch with my family and friends. Out of sight, out of mind. Occasionally, I would write a mass email, which I called Broadcast News—writing about exciting scenes celebrity adventures, hanging out in the rehearsal hall watching the Ceili dancers, the brilliant people who perform the traditional Irish dance at social gatherings, house parties, rural country side and now, in our film.

Again an email from Dick saying the fierce depression frightened him.

I called him. *"What's going on, Dick?"*

"There's no work, Jude. Nothing. My phone is dead."

"Aren't your regular clients working?"

"They must be. But not with me."

And then, without considering his feelings, I said a really stupid thing. *"I've been giving a great deal of thought to closing our office, Dick. Both of us can work independently. We have for the past few years."*

There was dead silence on his end of the phone and then... *"But what about all we created? The hundreds of films and commercials we worked on, with huge success? What about our crew...the grips and electricians we taught and brought up through the ranks. What about the creatives who loved our work? What about them?"* he pleaded.

"We have to look at facts, Dick, even though I still send money back to the company, I kind of resent it. I'm the one on the front lines making the films. You do commercials. We should work independently. No one calls Central Casting for me anymore, they just call me directly. Like they call you directly."

"Except no one calls me anymore, Judy."

Ever the cheerleader...*"That will change, Dick. It always does. You're just in a temporary dry spell. Are you still feeling depressed?"* I asked.

"Yes."

"Dick...listen to me. Get to a doctor and get on antidepressants. Get a therapist. Now. Sometimes it takes the meds a few weeks to kick in. You need help now and you probably won't need the medication for long," I announced.

"Judy, I've been clean and sober for sixteen years. If you

think I'll start taking pills now you are fucking nuts. Conversation closed."

"OK, Dick. But what about your depression? How are you dealing with it?"

"It's getting better," he lied. *"I'm hanging in there.*

"If you could just please keep sending back the fifteen percent to the company that would be great."

"Of course, I will. We'll get through this together and discuss any changes to the company when I'm home. Just promise me you'll see a doctor. Now, you've reinvented your career plenty of times before. This is just one of those dark times. You have a lot of goodness in your life, a lot to be grateful for. Call friends, meet them for lunch and let them pick up the tab. Keep going to your meetings and confide in Karen.

"You promise me you'll take care of yourself, Dick? I need you on the planet."

"I'm doing the best I can, Jude," he said. I decided to believe him.

We wrapped filming in Chicago at the end of May. After eight months in the windy city, I was definitely ready to head back to Los Angeles where we had The last scenes to shoot.

Chicago to LA. American Airlines. Away we go.

After a few days of prepping the Los Angeles locations, fitting the extras in period clothing, and cutting their hair, we were ready to film. The end of the movie, the final wrap, was just around the corner!

We were on the back lot at Warner Bros., Hennessy Street. It was a sticky hot Burbank afternoon. Vapor rose from the street as the mostly male crew prepared for the final scene we began that night. The death scene.

The crew tested the rain towers and wind machines. Flying

water cooled down the acrid air but only for a moment. Instead of smelling like sweet summer childhood rain, that rain smelled of diesel; dirty, thick. I was hot and tired. My thin hair stuck against my neck, my stomach bloated and my back ached.

We were a busy little group—exhausted from all these months of being rigidly on point, shooting in Chicago and finally we were back in California and preparing for the final scenes.

Leaving Chicago, I boarded in the first group so I got my favorite seat in the exit row where indeed I knew how to open that door. I am very, very good in an emergency.

I'm exactly who you want to be sitting next to on the airplane. I am a fixer. Always have been. Until June 14.

We were milling about, anxiously waiting for the sun to set so we could start rolling camera. We'd rehearsed this scene to death, pun intended. Finally ready. I was uncomfortable because this was a killing scene, but I was safely removed because it's just a movie, show business, not real. We are overpaid grown-ups taking pictures of someone else's 'death.' Safely, smugly removed from any semblance of real life we slouched in director's chairs sipping cappuccino watching stunts and FX worked with the stars, making sure they hit their marks as the squibs sent black red blood flying on cue toward the camera.

Over and over Tom Hanks blasted his screaming staccato Tommy gun into the air. Over and over Paul Newman crumbled onto the slick street—his pretend blood mixing with pretend rain. Over and over the director said, "More blood, please. Thank you. Step out. And action! Cut. Print. Very good, everyone. Print that one. Just one more, please." And the clean-up crew ran in with their wet vacs and quickly sucked up all the messy debris that naturally accompanies 'death.' They worked fast. In a matter of minutes, we were ready to 'kill' again.

84

We laughed and joked between takes. It was two a.m., three a.m., four a.m. I had continuous cappuccino as Tom repeatedly 'killed' Paul. I was tired, bored and slightly pissed off because some of the fake blood had landed on my new jeans.

And so, preoccupied as I was with our little death drama I was completely unprepared for the life-changing voice on the other end of my cell phone. At the very moment, we were 'killing' for *DreamWorks*, I received a call from San Luis Obispo in Central California.

"Is this Ms. Bouley?"

"Yes. How can I help?"

"We're looking for information on Dick Broder."

"Why? What kind of information? Who are you?"

"I'm a detective. I received a call from Mr. Broder's wife this morning. Mrs. Broder called to tell us he seems to have gone missing."

"Dick isn't missing!" I declared. *"He's location scouting for a Honda commercial. I spoke to him two days ago after he shot sunrise at the Pinnacles."*

"His wife said he didn't call her last night like he always does."

"I'm sure he just fell asleep after his long day out in the sun, driving and photographing lots of picturesque places."

"We just spoke with the producer of the commercial who said she hadn't heard from Mr. Broder either and that he always called her at the end of his day."

"There's a perfectly reasonable explanation for this," I said. *"Dick probably got a flat tire. He's useless with tools. He may have spent the night up in the hills smoking Marlboros and chewing gum. Maybe he got his car stuck on a rock. He's probably just waiting for a ranger to stumble onto him. There's*

no cell reception up there."

"OK, we'll send a ranger to look for him. Do you know where he might be?"

"Yes, he almost always photographs up in the Pinnacles in Monterey County. That's a big area. Helicopter may be the way to go."

"OK. Thanks for your help. I'll be in touch."

"I'm sure he's cold and dying for a cup of coffee but as long as he has his cigarettes and bubble gum he'll make it."

I called Dick's wife Karen. She answered the phone crying hysterically, *"He's never silent like this. He always calls at the end of his day."*

"He's fine, Karen. I know it. He's probably had car trouble. You'll hear from him any minute." I decided and prayed I was correct.

"The producer hasn't heard from him either!"

"I know. I just got off the phone with the producer. Are you alone, Karen?"

"No. Two of my girlfriends are sitting with me. They'll stay as long as I need them to."

"Good. We'll all sit tight until the detective calls us with good news. I promise everything will be fine," I promised. I'm a fixer.

I called Dick's phone five times. Each time I got the message that the phone was not working. I said a prayer that Dick would be safe and then I went back to work. More gunfire and blood, more clean-up crew with their wet vacs.

Two hours later, the detective called. *"I need to tell you something, Ms. Bouley."*

Words I will never forget.

And Detective Steve Something told me that in room 314 of

the Pismo Beach Inn, a small hotel room with no ocean view, my sweet partner and best friend of fourteen years sat in his morning clothes, his soft green sweatpants, faded and rumpled, smelling of Marlboros—and put a fully loaded cold .357 Magnum revolver filled with hollow-point bullets against his fifty-seven-year-old tired, terrorized forehead.

And in one swift, terrible, unrehearsed instant, Dick pulled the trigger.

One take. I'm the clean-up crew. How in God's name was I going to fix this?

It Takes a Village

"Happiness comes when your work and words
are of benefit to yourself and others."
– Buddha

6,700 feet about sea level in the Lesser Himalayas, blanketed over lush verdant hillsides, Darjeeling, India is a paradise of colonial charm, Hindu and Buddhist culture and kind, beautiful people. The snow-covered peaks of Kangchenjunga, the third-largest mountain in the world, loom high over Darjeeling and Nepal.

Darjeeling, India—an oasis, a contradiction, a lesson in humanity and grace.

We shot Peter Weir's ferocious film, *The Way Back*, in Bulgaria, Morocco, and India. Based on a compilation of true stories, *The Way Back* tells the unbelievable true story of five men who break out of a Russian gulag in 1941 and walk over four thousand miles through Siberia, China, Mongolia, and Tibet to finally arrive in India. Included in the cast of prisoners are: Colin Farrell, Ed Harris, and Jim Sturgess. On their tortuous journey, they meet a young Polish girl played fiercely by sixteen-year-old Irish actor Saoirse Ronan.

The morning walk to my casting office was my favorite part of the day. I passed through the chaotic Chowk Bazaar, a flea market business district, usually stopping to search for items from sellers in their rickety wooden square stalls selling everything from primary colored plastic kitchenware to children's dresses, underwear, shoes, rakes, tools, and packaged food. My favorite were the shawls, patterned or solid-colored, cotton or Kashmir. All exquisite. Brown-faced women with huge smiles, holding sleeping babies would call out to me, "Hello, madam!"

Again, I felt part of a community.

My twenty-minute walk on mud streets took me past tiny and medium-sized businesses. Skinny dogs lay in a pile, one lying on top of the other. Hundreds of shoddy electric lines hung crisscross, dangerously close to tin buildings or lay in rain puddles on broken asphalt streets. Packs of children dressed in grey and navy uniforms, wearing dark blue ties, carried bulging backpacks to school. Unbelievably, scrawny men wearing rags carried ridiculously huge loads of *anything* on their backs, held in place by a kerchief tied around the item and their head. One man carried a chair, another a small refrigerator!

Day one, I arrived at a subterranean two-room office carpeted in dirty brown with one wooden desk and a worn blue couch in the main room. The second room up I set up as the video recording room where my auditions would take place.

"Welcome to India," said my assistant, Sanjeev. Young and eager, I fell in love with him immediately. I sensed that working as my assistant on such a genius film would change his life forever. Turns out I was right.

After, "Hello, it is an honor to meet you!" Sanjeev said. "Will I be able to meet Mr. Peter Weir? To watch him work?"

"Of course," I said.

"Bless you, madam," Sanjeev said, and we went to work.

Using the toilet was a great adventure! Housed in a tiny room with no roof, the toilet was a hole in the ground with two muddy

89

indentations on either side where you place your feet. Once steady, you squat. Next to the hole in the ground was a bucket holding questionable water. After you did your business, you scooped water and cleaned yourself. I'm petite and a great squatter. The toilet hole didn't faze me one bit. It reminded me of growing up in our small village in Japan.

We were always squatting!

My lifesaver in Darjeeling, besides my Sanjeev, was Mr. Gurung, who was involved with the local theatre. He arranged for the local actors to meet with me. A teacher brought classes of well-dressed and well-behaved school children to auditions.

One special boy, a ten-year-old orphan named Bicky, was my favorite. Peter featured him with extreme close-ups many times.

Mr. Gurung, Sanjeev, and I met for tea at the Mayfair Hill Hotel in Darjeeling. Built in 1927 as the Maharasha's summer palace, the Mayfair served as our cast and crew hotel.

Mr. Gurung understood that we needed to cast an entire village, from the ages of six to eighty-five. We had two weeks to get everyone cast and costumed. While a handful of us prepped India, our crew was filming in Morocco, cheating it for the Gobi Desert. The plan was the day after the crew arrived in Darjeeling we would shoot. Ambitious, but indeed the entire movie was.

Mr. Gurung's gems kept pouring in: local policemen, a Hindu priest, tiny happy children, sun-wrinkled men and women, brown and bent in their eighties, and a small, old peasant woman who roasted corn in the street over a fire pit.

"Sanjeev," I said, "we need to go to the tea estate and meet with the women who pick the tea leaves. The scene calls for them to be scattered along the hillside harvesting the crop."

"I'll get the driver," Sanjeev said.

And off we went. On our hour drive to the village, as our driver told us the history of the terraced hillside tea estates created by the British in 1856.

We climbed the lush verdant hillside and watched the process—small women, wearing wicker baskets over their backs, many with children strapped on their chest, spent the day stooped over, picking green leaves from the bushes.

For a few rupees a day, they picked the leaves, for eight hours each day that make the famous Darjeeling tea, consumed across the globe. At the end of their shift, the pickers would return to the main building—an open-air wooden structure where each woman climbed wooden stairs taking their full baskets to the weigh stations. At the top of the stairs, two men standing behind scales had each woman empty her basket onto one. For the leaves they had picked that day, the women received their small allotment of rupees for their work in the scorching sun. The man who ran the tea estate took a portion of the women's rupees.

Once we had signed people up for the film, it was time to costume them. For that exercise, we rented a secondary school which was empty due to summer break.

I ran to Joe Cigliano, our brilliantly talented costumer. "Joe, I've got this exquisite mother and child…a real Madonna. She's probably nineteen and her baby maybe three. Her beautiful face is exquisitely and permanently sunburnt brown. The child is serene, innocent. They're perfect for us!"

"Peter will love them! Here's the rub. Our Costume Supervisor, Bridget doesn't have anything in our color palette small enough to fit him. Can he wear his own white pajamas?"

"Absolutely not. You know white bounces off the lights."

"I know but please? We have to have them!"

"Judy, get real. You know we have to costume these

villagers in our color palette. Only pastels, tan, beige, and cream. I did not say the word white."

"They have to be in the movie, Joe! I know we made all the costumes but can we buy something for him?" Joe takes a long drag on his cigarette. Then another. "Joe, Peter will go nuts for them. I promise. They're iconic. A perfect visual."

"Let me talk to the tailors and see what we can do."

"This is why I adore you," I reply, loving that, like normal, I get my way. I head back to my 'casting office,' which is a shoddy classroom with dirt floors, a tiny chalkboard and four pieces of broken chalk. My assistant was a sixteen-year-old girl, a student at the secondary school where we were costuming and photographing out eclectic cast. Each villager would come in, sign a register mostly by drawing an X for their signature and would go down the hall to our costume department—the community room at the school. There our Costumer Supervisor, Bridget Ostershelte, and her local crew had hung on racks: peasant clothing, skirts, loose-fitting trousers and long-sleeved shirts and blouses, traditional Kurti for men and Kurta for women all designed perfectly by our Costume Designer, Wendy Stites, Peter's wife and amazing creative partner.

Joe thought for a moment and left to huddle with the talented film tailors we had imported from Mumbai. Moments later, Joe was standing out in a field stirring dye and muslin in a sawn-off half-rusty barrel. Soon, huge pieces of beige muslin hung from over the wooden rail from the second story of the school.

While the muslin dried, one of our crew—a tailor from Mumbai, made a pattern from the little boy's white pajama. From that, he created, in about twenty minutes, cream-colored loose-fitting bottoms and top. Perfect. Mother and Child. Peter featured them in the opening scene in India.

After the boy was costumed, his mother cried from happiness. I paid her their rupees for coming to their fitting. She and her precious son. She signed by putting her X on the signature line. "You are paid more rupees on the day of shooting," I announced. I want to hand out lots of rupees in this poor village. Once costumed, each villager came back to me to be photographed. With each unique face (and heart) I saw the scene grow. *How many hours till I can show Peter the photos?* I calculated.

The Way Back 'village' we created included: infants, children ages three to ten, Bicky, our special boy Peter featured. Adults of all ages and professions: leaf pickers from the tea estate, an unmarried and childless teacher who cared for Bicky, a nine-year-old orphan, merchants, unemployed women and men, an attorney, tea pickers, an eighty-year-old musician, a Hindu priest, and more. OUR Village.

On the first morning of filming on the hillside of the tea estate, the priest blessed the director, cinematographer, myself, and others in the crew. He blessed our camera. He did this with a prayer, burning incense, an offering of rice and flowers, and soft red clay he smudged onto our third eye. As is Hindu custom, as a sign of respect, I bent down and touched his feet.

Once blessed, Peter began setting up the first shot.

Oh Shit! Here Comes a Cyclone

And...Action!
– Peter Weir, Director

Please get out of my bra, madam.
– Judith Bouley, Casting Director, Author

The horrific cyclone hit our village twenty-four hours before we began filming.

No one saw it coming. Our director and our producer, Duncan Henderson, huddled with our director to make a decision as to whether or not we would shoot the next day. Peter took Duncan's wise decision to push our call time (when we arrive on set) by only one hour. It was the perfect solution.

We drove the one-hour drive from our hotel to the set to our tea estate. Unbelievably, ninety-nine of our background actors arrived at base camp, though some had lost their tiny wooden and tin homes. A catered breakfast was served to all. Then Bridget and Joe had them all get into their costumes. It was a true celebration.

Peter arrived, looked at everyone, and gave me a huge hug. I was thrilled that he was thrilled. Duncan hugged me next. I hugged all hundred of our precious extras and we went to set.

Our first shot was on the steep, terraced hillside. A handful of women, with their toddlers, were shielded from the sun stooped under brown cone-shaped baskets.

One mother breastfed her tiny baby. They ate rice from small tin bowls.

Peter called action and the baskets were slowly lifted. The women were startled and curious. En masse, they stared at the top of a distant hillside. There, three men, leaning on walking sticks, were unrecognizable with scraggly beards concealing their sunburnt faces.

They walked slowly, bent over in the heat.

Peter featured a young boy, about ten, Bicky, the orphan child I cast. One of the women sent him running down the hill to tell a villager who was riding a horse. The man galloped away to tell the village elder and others.

Soon, the women on the hill and the entire village ran to see the men who by that time had made it down the hillside through the tea leaves. Their faces were hidden by filthy rags. The villagers walked slowly. A curious stream headed toward the men. The men, astonished, picked up their pace to meet the crowd.

The police chief led the way. He was followed by the village elder who sat perched on a wooden rickshaw carried by four men. The police chief welcomed the men. The three men asked, in sign language, if they could walk with them. All looked at the elder who nodded his approval. The villagers surrounded the men, shaking their hands, touching their clothes, bowing to them with respect. A group of small children made circles around the men

Three of them, giggling, held their hands. Finally, the men found freedom.

The lead man, played by the delicious actor Jim Sturgess, drew, with a stick in the dirt, the treacherous journey they had taken. Unbelievably, the three men had walked over four thousand miles through Siberia, China, Mongolia, and the Gobi

Desert, finally to arrive in India.

It was Peter and Duncan's plan to shoot for only one day. Apparently, the weather gods didn't get the memo. We were fogged in. Again. We shot day two. No luck. Day three we got it!

There were hugs, kisses, and tears as we wrapped out last day. I had given eight months of my life to *The Way Back*. I'd do it again in a heartbeat.

Heavy silence in the vans as we returned to our hotel. Our wrap party that night was bittersweet. After eight months together, our film family was dissolving. We hugged and kissed each other, promised to stay in close touch, and went to our rooms to finish packing.

Sadly, it was time to leave. After one night at the Leela Hotel in New Delhi, I was driven to the airport to head back to my home in Northern California. I waited in the wretched hot queue to get through immigration. The putrid stench of humanity, curry, and urine made my stomach rumble.

I just needed to get through immigration, which I was pretty nervous about, and get on Virgin Airlines to San Francisco.

I came to the front of the line. The officer stared at me, then my passport, then at me again. "How long were you in India, madam?"

"Two weeks, sir."

He pulled on his black mustache. "What was the purpose of your trip?"

"I was working on a film in Darjeeling."

His mood lifted as he exclaimed, "I love the movies. Titanic, with the ship, with Leo!"

"Yes, sir," I replied. "I did not work on that."

"Too bad," he replied. "Great movie."

And he stamped my passport.

I was home free. What I hadn't planned on was the young woman who told me she was going to give me a body search. Shit! "May I keep my clothes on, madam?" I begged.

"Of course, madam. But it will be a full body search." Uh oh. Was this going to be just like *Midnight Express?*

She had me remove my shoes, felt my feet, and moved her hands up my legs. She got to my groin, and I was hoping she'd respect me in the morning. My stomach passed her inspection, and finally, she passed her hands lightly over my breasts. She looked confused. I have full breasts, but that day they had a bit of padding.

"Madam! Is that your brassiere?"

Of course, it is," I replied. "It feels rather strange. Follow me, please, madam. I will need you to remove your brassiere so I may inspect it." *And Bullshit,* I thought, *she's not getting to second base with me. Not without dinner and drinks!*

Finally, I came clean. "Madam," I began, "please forgive me. I admit that I am carrying ten thousand dollars in cash. Five thousand in each bra cup. I protest that I can legally take ten thousand dollars out of India."

"That is correct, madam. Most people simply put their cash in their baggage."

Sheepishly, I said, "I understand, madam, and I sincerely apologize. May I please go through now? My plane will leave soon."

She looked me up and down, smiled, and said, "Madam, be sure to stop at the gift shop on your way out. Please come back to India."

I thanked her, in Hindi. "*Dhanyavaad*, madam." I bowed and said, "*Namaste.*" (I honor the God within you, a standard Hindi

97

greeting.) I waved goodbye to her and said a silent prayer of thanks to India. I said goodbye to all the magic we had created and loved in this stunning, perplexing country. Then I went straight to the gift shop, bought three pashminas and a small Buddha.

Dog tired, teary, sad to leave and excited to return home, I boarded Virgin Air.

Off to my next grand adventure. Rinse. Repeat.

We Need Mongolians!

"You're not going to Kazakhstan, Judy, you can't even spell that."
– Duncan Henderson, Amazing human, Producer, my dear friend.

Sofia, Bulgaria, winter, 2009. Our film crew is bundled up in the best REI and Patagonia outerwear money can buy to film in blizzards for exterior shots and on stage, which was just as cold, for interior shots, for the iconic director, Peter Weir's epic film *The Way Back*. Peter, using his heart as one of his camera lenses, guided our amazing cast: Colin Farrell, Ed Harris, Jim Sturgess, and the very young, as yet undiscovered, fifteen-year-old Saoirse Ronan.

Our story is set in 1941. Six men break out of a gruesome Siberian prison camp in the dead of winter and begin a four-thousand-mile journey, on foot, hoping to find freedom. They cross unforgiving Siberia, China, Mongolia, the Gobi Desert, and finally arrive in India. (Spoiler alert if you haven't seen the film, not all of them make it).

We're well into filming, and my next assignment is to search for five excellent horseback riders, ages ten to fifty, who appear to be Mongolian and are free to fly to Morocco with us as we are cheating Morocco for the Gobi Desert. Piece of cake.

I walk down the hall of our studio, Nu Boyana, which was built during Soviet times. It's one huge four-story square concrete structure built around a courtyard. Our offices are small and cold. Some of us work in fingerless gloves. It's snowing outside, a bleak Bulgarian winter, with almost no light coming in through the windows.

I head to my producer's office. Duncan Henderson is the finest producer I have ever worked with. He is whip-smart, funny, has a heart of gold, and decades of experience. Duncan doesn't suffer fools lightly. I always make sure I can defend whatever I'm asking for.

I plop down on the chair next to his desk. "Hey, Duncan, how's your day going? I gotta go to Kazakhstan."

He looks up from his computer and says, "What?"

"Kazakhstan. It's a country to which I have to go."

"You're not going to Kazakhstan, Judy. You can't even spell that."

He's got a point but I don't budge.

"Duncan, as you know, I need to cast four men and one young boy who appear to be Mongolian for a few scenes in the film, which we'll shoot in Morocco."

"Yes, Judy. I'm aware. What does this have to do with Kazakhstan?"

"I found the boy there! He was the stunt rider for the child in *Mongol*, the ferocious film by Sergei Bodrov. The boy's father owns a horse riding school. This will be a slam dunk."

Duncan says I can go to Kazakhstan.

"*Spasiba*," I say, which means thank you in Russian.

"You're welcome," Duncan says.

"That's *pozhaluysta*!" I reply.

"I don't care. Have Marina get tickets and visas ready for you and Kala. Make sure your cell phone will work there so you can check in with me."

100

I reach into my bag, pull out two tickets, and smile.

"Judy, you already had Marina get your tickets before you came into my office?"

"Yes, sir. I did. Just doing my job."

There's a beat.

"Anything else, Miss Bouley?"

"*Ah*, yup. Just a heads-up, Kala and I will also be going to Kyrgyzstan. There's a ton of horseback riders I've arranged to meet there. They look very Mongolian!"

"Get out of my office, Judy."

"Copy that, Duncan. I love you."

"I know you do. Call me from Kazakhstan and Kyrgyzstan. Just call me from all the Stans. I love you too, now go away."

"Yes, boss!" I replied. And off we went.

Our stunt coordinator, Kala, speaks Russian. I don't. So I invited him on the excursion. We board the plane in Sofia and deplane in Almaty. On approach, Kala says to me, "Judy, there will be a man at immigration with a very big gun. Don't look at him or speak to him."

"Why not?" I ask.

"Because he won't have a sense of humor."

I'm not a fan of being told what to do so the second I'm off the plane, I walk up to the boy strapped to a Kalashnikov.

"*Privet*," I say to him which is hello in Russian.

He doesn't reply. I try to hug him but he pushes me away and points his rifle in my general direction. Kala rushes between the two of us and probably said, "She's a crazy American."

We get our visas and walk out of the airport where our host, the very kind Mr. Tursingaliev greets us, and takes us to his horse riding academy where he teaches stunts on horses. The lads are all on point on their horses as we arrive. I grab my camera and climb to the top of the wooden fence so I have a great view. The men parade in front of me.

I film it all.

The young boy, Termirkhan Tursingaliev, gallops past me. He is stunning. Peter must have this child. When the men have stopped riding I've selected two of them to join the young boy and go with us to film in Morocco. Mr. Tursingaliev invites Kala and me to a delicious lunch. Afterward, Kala and I go to our hotel. Kala goes to the bar. I go to my room to edit the footage I shot to show Peter and Duncan.

Mr. Tursingaliev invites us to go to a nightclub with him. I drink wine. The men drink vodka. I dance. They don't. Kala flirts. We leave after midnight. At the elevator, Kala and I say goodnight. Just as I'm falling asleep, there is a knock on my door. I answer the door and find a young, scantily clad beautiful woman surprised to see me. I point down the hall to Kala's door.

The next day, we flew to Kyrgyzstan where we meet with a very well-to-do rancher who owns many horses. Standing in a huge field, the men ride by me. Some stand on their horses and ride right toward my lens.

My eye is against the eyepiece of my camera. Kala is next to me to protect me from the horses charging at me. Kala tells me to stop filming and look to my right where a sheep is giving birth to a lamb!

I hire my last two riders, a father and son, and my work is finished.

The next day, Kala and I fly back to Sofia. I show Peter the footage and, like me, he's thrilled.

Kazakhstan, Kyrgyzstan. I couldn't spell, pronounce, or find them on a map. But I damn sure went there and found the most amazing Mongolian horse riders for our film. Peter, Duncan, and I were over the moon.

Dante's Inferno

*"And through thick woods, one finds a stream astray so
secret that the very sky seems small. I think I will not hang
myself today."*
– GK Chesterton

Many years into my stunning, non-stop career, I began to get
sick. Not because of it.

Rather, it was a perfect storm of life-altering events. I lived
for years like a Bedouin, film to film, on location, overworking
everywhere; combined with the wrong lovers *(or, mostly the lack
of)* left me up in the air. I couldn't find my feet or foundation.
Balance? I'd survived too many deaths of dear family and
friends. One suicide. I had always thought that at some point in
my later years, I'd work as a volunteer for Hospice. Who knew
that would happen so early in my life? I lost my dear Uncle Al,
best friends: Carol, Chuck, Maryellen, and Dick. And with each
death, I lost a piece of myself. I'd defined myself through my
close relationships and now here I was, being slowly chipped
away. Dick and his .357 Magnum, the chamber fully loaded with
hollow-point bullets. Me: the clean-up crew. Like that.

Physical and existential exhaustion combined with my
spiritual apartheid led me to quicksand, getting sucked down
further into my personal version of Dante's inferno, the dark
night of the soul, indeed. My attempts to claw my way out of the
abyss failed. And then my phone rang.

"Hey, sis. How are you?" my sister, Sandi asked.

"I'm OK," I lied.

"Really?"

"No," I admitted.

"Right. I didn't think so."

I spent some more minutes trying to convince us both I was fine. 'Just having a bad day,' but I couldn't even pull the pop top on the Ensure vanilla supplement I was sort of drinking as my weight had dwindled to scarecrow category. I couldn't muster the energy or concentration to write my rent check or finish the suicide note I'd begun. Finally, I had to admit I was sinking further down the rabbit hole as each stupid sunrise occurred.

"Jude, what's happening to you? Where did you go? Where's my sister?"

"Sandi. Everyone just has to be patient with me. I'm getting stronger! I'm gonna do another movie soon!" I announced. *"I just need to get back in the saddle and I'll feel like me again! I just need an airplane ticket to somewhere."*

"Sis. You can't do a movie now. You're not even feeding yourself. Mom says you call her every morning to come over to babysit you because you're scared to be alone. She said when she arrives, you're kneeling on the floor rocking back and forth. Then you take sleeping pills and go back to bed. Mom said you can't even drive anymore! You're not having a bad day, sis. You're having a bad life right now. You need help to turn yourself around. Clearly, you can't do this on your own anymore. Mom is scared. So am I. The whole family is."

Silence. Then I cry.

"OK. I'll be there in two days," Sandi said. And she was. My big sister boarded a plane and flew from her home on the Big Island of Hawaii to come and save little tiny me in Santa Cruz.

We spent a few days researching hospitals, mental health clinics, groovy yoga feel-good group therapy places for $10,000 a week (!) skipped that, and on my sage therapist cousin's advice, called the world re-nowned Menninger Clinic in Houston. I had a phone interview, which I passed when I mentioned I was suicidal.

"I won't actually take my own life," I assured the intake counselor. *"I'm a Buddhist. It's just that...if I can't think my way out of this terror it's probably my best default."*

She disagreed. *"Judy, I know our doctors can help you get healthy. May I please have your credit card number, expiration date, and security code on the back? We accept Visa, Mastercard, and American Express. I'm happy to hold."*

Forms and instructions were sent to me. Included in them was a list of what I should and shouldn't pack. No sharp objects or razor blades, no valuables, no work of any kind, no cell phone, no nail files. I didn't have the strength or thinking to pack so my sister and my cousin, Lisa did that for me. Two days later, we boarded Southwest Airlines and headed to Houston, Texas where I climbed onto Mr. Toad's wild ride.

Mister Toad's Wild Ride

*"He who jumps into the void owes no
explanation to those who stand and watch."*
– Jean-Luc Godard

"That's it mister. You just lost your brain privileges."
– SpongeBob SquarePants

A middle-aged man in rumpled pajamas pushed his hand through his greasy grey hair and swatted at a ping-pong ball that had flown by him and bounced on the stained blue carpet. An attendant in worn green scrubs retrieved the ball and put it in the man's hand. Then ping-pong guy cried.

Another inmate, agitated, waited at the opposite end of the table. Pushing seventy, unshaven, he wrung his hands, muttering to himself. It looked to me like a ball game was the last thing on these gents' minds.

"I'm not staying here," I announced to Sandi.

"Oh yes, you are, sis. We can't help you at home. You're severely depressed. You need proper treatment. This clinic is one of the best in the country."

"I'm not a crazy person," I pleaded. *"I've done four movies with Tom Hanks. I can sing and dance in Japanese, order food and book the train in French and Spanish. I've owned two homes and raised money for the Peace Corps to build a school in Manila when I was in ninth grade!"*

"No one said you're not accomplished, sis, but right now, for whatever reason, your brain is shutting down and these guys are going to fix you. You're going to buck up and do their program. It's just for a few weeks, until you're stronger."

"Sandi," I said. *"Listen to my words. I. Am. Not. Staying. In. A. Looney Bin. With. Ping. Pong. People."*

"Yes. You. Are," she decreed. *"Yes, you are, yes you are, yes you are...infinity!"* It was our childhood game. Whoever called 'infinity' first won.

With a warm hug and whispered reassurances that my life would soon be right side up, my sister left. So then I hated her. A young, pretty black woman, the charge nurse wearing a plastic name badge with Sheila typed on it led me to my room consisting of two single beds and one wacky roommate who paced around piles of clothes strewn all over the floor. She stepped on underwear, prodded through it with her left foot then let out a squeal and hopped from foot to foot. Then paced again. Back and forth, back and forth. He toed more piles, squealed. *Oh fuck me.* And this was just day one.

I turned to Sheila and leaned my head to the right, twice, indicating my roommate, the pacer, and raised my hands, palms up, in question. Sheila smiled and nodded. *Which means, what, exactly?* Then she lifted my suitcase to a bed. That's when I noticed my bed had a plastic sheet covering the mattress.

"I'm not a puppy," I said to Sheila. "Potty trained at two!"

"That's just to keep things sanitary, ma'am," she replied in a slow, southern sing-song. Item by item Sheila rooted through my suitcase removing the bits I wasn't allowed to keep: my nail file, cell phone, a brown plastic headband. Apparently, at the looney bin, 'head-banding' myself to death was verboten.

The 'bin' is Menninger Clinic, a big deal treatment facility affiliated with Baylor University in Houston, Texas. Fancy, smart, world-class pedigreed professionals worked there: doctors, psychiatrists, psychologists, nursing staff, and the guy who dusts the ping-pong table. Menninger is a locked facility. The brown brick ranch-style 'campus' as it is called, houses many patients with various disabilities and illnesses including severe depression and anxiety disorders, post-traumatic stress syndrome, bulimia and anorexia, schizophrenia, drug and alcohol addiction. At my intake interview, or as I like to think of it, 'my audition,' I picked up a pamphlet that quotes the Senior Vice President and CEO of the clinic: "We know that our intensive collaborative treatment with a team of specialists enables patients to regain a healthy level of functioning and to stay well after returning home."

I looked straight at the intake counselor. "Do you guys take American Express?"

The program I was in was called Professionals in Crisis which accepts twenty-two patients for six weeks. During my stay, my comrades in crazy included the CEO of a Fortune five hundred corporation who told me he paid $40,000 for his Rolex (which *proves* he's nuts), a dentist from Seattle, a writer/director from The New School in New York City (his Oscar-winning girlfriend just dumped him), and eight physicians, six of whom had attempted suicide by swallowing pills and slicing some of their veins. *Medicine is apparently not a healthy career choice.* Toss in a gorgeous, chain-smoking, twenty-something lad with degrees from Harvard, a trust fund, and great hair and me. Professionals in crisis, indeed.

We attended mandatory classes on how the brain functions. On the menu: 'Know your Cerebral Cortex,' 'Stop Sucking Your Adrenals Dry,' 'The Limbic System: Emotions, Learning and

Memory,' and 'Amygdala Art!' Wherein we were given poorly photocopied drawings of the amygdala and a plastic container with colored pencils. I didn't want to color a picture of the amygdala, the part of the limbic system in my brain which is responsible for emotions, survival instincts, and memory. I just wanted mine fixed. For nine hundred dollars a day, I figured they could do that. Who wants to be able to remember emotions and survival instincts? I clearly remember mine kicking in at age five. Who wants to remember episodic bad choices by my precious and imperfect parents? *Did these guys read their job descriptions?* The dangerous ignorance of breaking boundaries, corporal punishment, alcoholism and molestation. What's the point? My theory: Shit happens. Move on.

First stop was an interview with my psychiatrist, Dr. Nguyen, a pedigreed, well-published shrink from UCLA. Her questions and my answers went like this:

Her: "Were you ever molested?"

Me: "Yes, by my grandfather when I was eleven years old."

Her: "Were you ever raped?"

Me: "Yes. Twice. Once at gunpoint."

Her: "Very good."

Me: *Yeah, not so much.*

Her: "Have you had any abortions?"

Me: "Yes. Three."

Her: "How old were you?"

Me: "21 and I don't remember."

Three yes-s! I passed the test with flying colors.

I don't believe in medication. I figure if you have a psychological issue you should meditate more and volunteer. On that Dr. Nguyen and I disagreed. From my interview, she diagnosed I have severe depression and a mood disorder. She prescribed: Lithium, Lamictal, Seroquel, and Prozac. I had read *Prozac Nation* so I really didn't want to take that one. Or any of them. I ate pills in the morning and at night. Again, like in *One Flew Over the Cuckoo's Nest,* we inmates in our bathrobes lined up as Nurse Ratchet dispensed the dope. She gave us a little paper cup of water and watched us swallow. We had to open our mouths and lift up our tongues so she was certain we weren't faking it in order to flush the meds down the toilet. Did I mention that our toilets had no seats? We sat on the rim. Seriously. This was to prevent us from committing suicide by swallowing the seat. I paid $900 per day for this and I had rim impressions on my ass.

We were meant to eat three meals a day, whether we wanted to or not. For the first week, an aide sat next to me to make sure I chewed and swallowed. We were weighed twice a week. I didn't do so well, usually coming in around ninety-nine lbs. This resulted in Eddie, the southern black cook who never missed a meal saying, "Miss. Judy, you best stop eating those tuna salads and have you some of my friend catfish and curly fries. You need to get some meat on your little bones." By week two, it dawned on me that all I really needed to do was put rocks in my pockets on weigh-in days. That tipped the scales to one hundred and one lbs! I fooled 'em and kept eating salad.

We had to exercise. Everyday. One hundred and nine humid degrees in July in Houston is *exactly* when I wanted to run track.

I swatted at a volleyball a few times. Did eight pushups. The exercise I did love doing was stretching in the yoga class held once a week, in the evening, in the group therapy room. The instructor was a 'normy' (non-bin person), a young woman who spoke in a soothing voice. Thin as a paperclip, wearing black yoga pants, tie-dyed flowing cotton blouse, and a light pink

110

crystal necklace around her neck, she led us through relaxation poses. We ended with a short, guided meditation. I hated when class ended.

Twice a week, we met with our team. Dr. Nguyen, she of the 'drown you in dope' method, a perfectly coiffed a pasty white mid-west social worker girl who had blonde bouffant hair, fake nails, and spoke in whispers...?

And an older black nurse with ridiculous breasts she wanted you to rest against when you were sad.

I did, twice.

"Your diagnosis is bipolar two depression," Dr. Nguyen said.

"Nope," I announced. "I'm not having that! I am so not bipolar. What does bipolar mean?" I asked.

The staff exchanged glances as I folded my arms across my chest.

"In simple terms, it is a mood disorder. In your case, it is primarily depression. At times you move a bit too fast."

"I am depressed. Episodically," I said. "I'll give you that. You go spend twenty-five years on film sets and see how you do! But I don't have bipolar! And I'm going to look it up!"

"It's not important what your diagnosis is. For now, your attention is about being vigilant, taking your medication, and working the program here with people who are fiercely determined to help you."

"I'm not having bipolar! No matter what number it is," I said. And left the room.

Wednesday evenings we had 'Movie Night' in the big room. Fifteen or so bodies sat or laid on couches or on big pillows on the carpeted floor. An aide announced, "OK, let's take a vote on which movie y'all want to see."

111

"Castaway?"

No thanks, I made it.

"Perfect Storm?"

Nope...made that one too.

"Runaway Train?"

I didn't make that one, but I'd love to hop on.

The group chose *Castaway.* I whispered to the woman on my left, "The theme of this film is 'hanging on for dear life.'" I left the room immediately so I could do just that.

After our Trauma class, we attended Group Therapy. My first group therapy session went something like this: "Welcome to Menninger," the doctor said. He's British and his socks didn't match.

"Thanks!" I replied. "I hear people are practically dying to get in." Immediately I was sorry I piped up. I tried to shrink myself to invisible. I stared at his crossed legs. One sock red. One sock blue.

"OK," he responded. "Let's go with that for our first topic. Has anyone here ever contemplated or attempted suicide?" Nine hands go up, some with freshly bandaged wrists. I waited till all the hands have gone up and finally raise mine, halfway. "OK, Judy, let's begin with you." *Oh, let's don't.*

"Did you actually attempt suicide?"

"No," I said. "I chickened out."

"OK. Did you have a plan?"

"Yes."

"Would you mind sharing with the group what your plan was?"

Love to.

"I planned to drive my fully fueled vehicle to the Bixby Bridge on the Northern California Coast, and make a hard right,

112

toward Hawaii."

"And why do you think you didn't you do that?"

"It struck me as a waste of a perfectly good, high-performance German automobile," I deadpanned. I was going to win this crowd over if it was the last thing I did.

"OK. Anything else?"

"Yes. I couldn't get through the spell check on the third draft of my 'I'm sorry' letter."

The guy next to me whispers, "Me too! My spelling sucks."

The Brit sock doc nods. "OK. Thanks for sharing, Judy. Anyone else?"

Group Therapy met two times a week for one and a half-hour sessions. We went around the room and shared our stories. Some of us were rehearsed. That would be me, others extemporaneous. Some were pissed off, mute, or sobbing. One guy, a pudgy brunette, pretzeled around himself on a bean bag chair and always nodded off in a drugged stupor.

We learned that most of us are perfectionists, terrified of failure, and damn sure won't give up control because then we'd fall apart. We suck up responsibility that's not ours, and then resent that we must do this or that, or we're afraid not to. We beat the shit out of ourselves when we can't fix what's broken, real or imagined. It didn't matter that it isn't ours to fix, or that control is an illusion. Some of us had sloppy childhoods and all of us wish we weren't in group therapy in the looney bin. We wish we were back in our lives and that we had life back in us.

Reuniting with Dina

"It is when we are most lost that we sometimes find our truest friends."
– Snow White

I was freshly out of the looney bin, living for free in my dear brother's studio.

I was scared. I wasn't on a movie. I couldn't find my feet or my foundation. Incessantly, I went to the movies. I had my favorite seat. Often I'd leave one theatre and go to the next. My great escape. A large dark room, previews of upcoming attractions, and the feature. Fuck you, depression. The projector cast it's blue light. Heaven.

I was hungry. For a burrito. So I went to Planet Fresh, the best burrito place in downtown Santa Cruz…organic ingredients, delicious.

As I was ordering my chicken burrito, I noticed a woman sitting alone at a table by a window. She had red hair, big beautiful mischievous blue eyes, and was beautifully dressed in a brown turtleneck sweater and navy blue pants. Around her neck, she wore a long silver necklace, holding the masks of comedy and tragedy. She was a woman whom I had known years ago called Dina Babbitt. Thrilled to see her, I ran over to give her a hug, and she was equally delighted to see me.

I got my lunch and joined her. "Judy, you haven't changed a bit. How have you been and *where* have you been? I haven't seen

114

you in years!" Because of all my travels and my tendency to isolate on location (out of sight, out of mind), I had lost track of Dina for many years while on the road.

We sat at our feast and began catching each other up on our adventures during our long absence. Little did I know that this was the beginning of a new, closer, sorely needed relationship for us both.

Dina and I met in the early eighties at a local animation film festival. Taking an immediate liking to each other, we spent good time together, with our respective partners—her husband, Les, and my boyfriend at the time, John. They came to our house for great conversation and dinners of marinated crab caught that morning, crunchy French bread, cheese, and Chardonnay. Typically, we finished the whole thing off with cheesecake and cognac.

We spent hours 'at table'—getting to know each other through our stories of travel, film, and living in Hollywood versus life in Santa Cruz. Dina and Les had lived in Los Angeles for twenty-five years before moving to Bonny Doon, a small mountain community in Santa Cruz, after Les retired from his career as a producer on cartoons for Disney and other studios. John and I visited their home, which was filled with books in German, Czech, English, and French. Every inch of wall was covered with watercolor and oil paintings of portraits, landscapes, abstracts, and oddly, a scene from *Snow White and the Seven Dwarfs*, in which Dopey stands on another Happy's shoulders, both draped in a beige trench coat. Against a backdrop of lush green hills dotted with cartoon flowers and grazing cows, Snow White and Dopey dance. All these years later, I never forgot that painting.

Over lunch, in quick succession, I gave Dina my frequent

flyer film history since our last rendezvous: Buenos Aires (*Evita*), Los Angeles, New Mexico, Puerto Rico (*Contact*), Los Angeles, Memphis (*Castaway*), Baja, California (*Master and Commander*), and more.

I also gave Dina an oral snapshot of my recent six-week field trip to the looney bin in Houston. She listened without interruption and then… "Listen, Judy, you shouldn't waste your time on depression. There is too much to live for."

I began to defend myself. "Depression isn't a choice, Dina." Knowing her singular, incredible, impossible story, I said, "Weren't you depressed for all those years?"

"I didn't have the luxury of depression, Judy. I was too busy trying to stay alive."

Silently, I played with my silverware. Compare and despair. *Her pain was worse than mine.* I felt guilty and ashamed.

Dina changed the subject. "How long until you leave for your next movie?"

"My plan is to stay home this year. Get strong again and then get back to work on location."

"Oh, good. Then we have time to play! Do you like tooney?" she asked in her accented English.

"You mean tuna?" I replied.

"I mean tooney. I'm famous for my tooney.

"What's in it?"

"I'm not telling you."

"OK. How soon can I come?"

"Come tomorrow. Tooney at noon."

I left the burrito place. Thrilled! Intuitively, I felt that something wonderful would happen from my reconnection with Dina. I had no idea Dina would change my life forever.

116

Auschwitz

Where does one go to get out of hell?
To Auschwitz, of course.
– Judy Bouley, Casting Director, author

It's a new day. Dina and I are in her cozy kitchen nook. I push the record button and Dina, with a whip-smart memory, goes back in time.

"The driver arrives daily now. We have our routine."

"I awaken at five a.m. when the Blockaeldeste, the guard screams for us to arise. The slow ones are beaten. Climbing down from our cramped wooden pallets where seven bodies are crammed into space for four, we shuffle outside to stand in the patch of dirt they call 'the yard,' in front of our brick barrack. We are waiting to be counted. That is what we do. We stand, daily, for hours, at attention in snow or rain. One by one we say our number aloud, without making eye contact with the guard. 61016," I say.

"We are counted twice, once by the Blockaeldeste, a Jewish prisoner living in our barrack who is responsible for keeping track of who is dead and alive and then we are counted by an SS guard. Most days it is the brutal woman with her thick, worn wooden beating stick who leads her snarling dog on a leash of black leather. I worry for that dog."

"The SS officer arrives and checks the ledger where the Blockaeldeste has noted who has died in the night."

117

"I stand in line and watch, as I do most days, the newly dead thrown one on top of the other. Corpses stacked high on a wooden cart. Their skeletons unrecognizable. Arms and legs like pick-up sticks.

"And that is the beginning of my morning.

"The ledger is closed until tomorrow. Two emaciated prisoners pull the cart of the dead to the ovens as the jeep arrives to deliver me to Dr. Mengele's office where I will paint."

The morning of our next session, Dina said to me, "Judy, I'm worried about you."

"Why?" I asked. "Am I acting weird?"

"No weirder than normal." She laughed.

"So?" I say.

"I'm worried that by writing my story you will fall back into depression. I'm not holding anything back from you and I know some of it may be too horrible for you to hear. You need to be tsoops in your life."

Tsoops is a phrase in Dina speak. She said it means 'comforting oneself.' Not to be *comfortable*, she was quick to point out, but rather to wrap oneself in comfort. Tsoops could be used as a verb, as in: *"I'm lying in the hammock, tsoopsing myself."* Or as a response to hearing some great news, as in: "Oh my God! I just won the lottery!"

"Tsoops!"

"Stop worrying," I announced. "I won't get depressed. I won't ever get depressed again! I made a promise to myself (as if that would work). I'm doing everything the doctors said. I take my medication, eat well, exercise, sleep eight hours every night, meditate and go to support groups. And now I have a writing schedule. Don't worry, Dina. It's important for me to have our project. You sharing your singular, unbelievable against all odds

118

story with me gives meaning to my life again. Now please, let's get back to work."

This time it was Dina who pushed the button on the tape recorder. "OK."

Over four months, I recorded Dina's gruesome, hopeful, and surprisingly funny story which did indeed give meaning to my life. Sharing her story with me, I actually gained relief from my severe depression.

Who knew? To get out of my own hell...I went to Auschwitz.

Snow White and the Seven Dwarfs

"Tsoops yourself!"
– Dina Babbitt

The drive to Dina's home in Felton, a small enclave in the Santa Cruz Mountains with a population of 3300, was magnificent. Enormous redwood trees and twisting roads which often narrowed to one lane.

Arriving at Dina's, I honked my horn, and she came to open the large wooden gate, exposing her small white-washed storybook cottage. Red geraniums in clay pots hung outside the windows. An outdoor table and chairs sat in the middle of a redwood deck. Everywhere I looked, something was growing. There were bright salmon-colored potted roses in bloom…light pink geraniums, and French and English lavender spilling over the sides of the wine barrels they were planted in.

In her huge yard, a hammock hung between two monstrous redwood trees, with a prolific persimmon tree close by. Off to one side of the yard was a green and white striped love seat where we would sit, nap, and use as an outdoor office. Her profuse garden grew butter lettuce, carrots, tomatoes, zucchini, pumpkins, and green beans twisted on the short chain-link fence. Dina's creed, "You must always plant and tend to your garden. We nourish ourselves. I will never taste hunger again."

The inside of Dina's cabin looked as I'd imagined it: clean, compact, filled with her art. I noticed a light grey clay sculpture of a young girl. Her face looked serene.

The inscription read: *'Effie, age eleven, a ballerina.'* I would later learn that Effie was gassed in Auschwitz.

Dina was right. The tooney was delicious. Post-lunch, we had strong coffee with milk. I told her I had to choose my own cup. "Why?" Dina asked.

"Because I always choose my own cup."

"Oy. So choose."

After some perusal, I chose a delft blue and white, short rounded cup. I held it out to Dina.

As she poured coffee into it, she pronounced, "I deem this Judy's cup." And so it was.

"No one else can use it," I said.

"God forbid," came her reply. Drink out of it now. Dessert was Dina's special brownies with cranberries. I always ate two.

"So what now Doompshling?" Dina's nickname for me, translating loosely to 'my sweet little one.' Sometimes, when I was a dufus, she called me Doomschpatz, which translates to 'my sweet little one who is making me crazy.'

"What's next for you?"

"Well," I began, "I've decided to write."

"Fantastic! What will you write—a screenplay, a book?"

I reached for another brownie. "Actually, Dina. I want to tell your story."

"Why?" she asked. "Because no one has lived the unbelievable life you have. And your story needs to be told."

"Doompshling, many other people have tried writing about me and I hated everything they wrote."

"You won't hate what I write," I said.

"Why not?"

"Because I know you."

Dina sipped her coffee, shrugged, and said, "OK. Why not?"

Three days later, I placed my tape recorder on the table in the cozy kitchen nook, a tiny, intimate space holding a small wooden table and two chairs. Sitting at the table, you could reach out your hand and open the refrigerator.

"Let's get to work," Dina said, pouring coffee.

I pushed the start button on my tape recorder. "Dina, tell me about painting for the children."

"We're starting there?" she asked.

"Not at the beginning?" I shrugged.

"OK. You're the boss," she said. And began.

"Well, a friend of mine, Freddy Hirsch, who I knew from art school in Prague, quite a well-known painter at the time asked me to paint a mural on a concrete wall for a group of young children. Freddy had organized cans of tempura paint in bright colors, and a paintbrush. I began painting green hills with blooming cartoony flowers, cows grazing underneath a blue sky. I thought that would please the children. They were a group of all boys, some hardly old enough to be away from their mothers. The older ones cared for the young ones. I asked if there was anything else they wanted in the mural. In unison they replied, Snow White! Paint Snow White...from the movie. And so I did."

"What scene did you paint?" I asked.

"The scene with Snow White dancing with Dopey standing on Happy's shoulders, both of them draped in a long coat. Doc plays a tiny accordion. Bashful plays drums. Sneezy claps along and Sleepy snores. With tiny arms folded across his chest, Grumpy takes it all in."

"And then what happened?" I asked.

"Nothing special happened. I just went home."

Home for Dina and her mother, Yatchi, in 1941, was Camp

122

B: the 'family barrack' in the Nazi concentration camp, Auschwitz/Birkenau. They slept on a wooden pallet stacked on top of two other pallets. Seven women were crammed onto these pallets with one thin blanket to cover all of them.

When Dina returned to her mother, she told her how happy she was, how comforted she felt as she painted. It made her so happy to hold the brush, moving it on the concrete wall applying vivid colors, the smell of the paint, excited children clapping their hands, giggling with delight. All this took Dina out of the hell she was in even if just for a moment.

"Dinetchka," her mother scolded. *"You will get us killed! This is crazy behavior. You are forbidden to paint anything again. What were you thinking? Give me your word you will never do anything stupid like this again! You are looking for trouble for both of us!"*

"Mama, you don't understand." Dina cried. *"Painting is the one thing I can do for some peace. It takes me out of this hell, back into my life!"*

"Grow up, Dinetchka. Auschwitz is the world you live in now. Not art. There is nothing colorful here. Your word, Dina. Give it to me. Promise me you will never do anything that stupid again!"

Dina swallowed back tears and said, *"OK. I promise."*

"Do you want more coffee?" Dina asked.

I said, "Yes." And asked for another brownie. As she poured, I asked, "Dina, I don't understand. I can't grasp this. You were surrounded by endless torture and death! How could you have painted that mural on the wall of the children's barrack?"

"How could I not?" she replied.

I returned two days later, and over coffee, I told Dina I had written, first person, in her voice, the story of what happened after she painted the Snow White mural. She looked skeptical but nodded, and I began reading aloud.

"It is eight a.m. on a lightless freezing day in November. I am twenty, starving and terrified when a jeep arrives at our family camp, driven by a young officer. He is handsome, with blonde hair and blue eyes. In another time we may have laughed and flirted over a coffee. But this in not another time."

Politely, he asks me, "Are you 61016?" I nod yes.

"Then please get in the jeep."

My throat closes. Blood freezes in my veins. After carefully scraping mud from my shoes I step into the jeep.

As the officer drives, I stare at the grey sky punctuated by dozens of chimneys, the brick buildings, the black boots of the SS guards strolling past rotting corpses. I stare at the endless line of skeletons slowly marching by, stooped over, carrying rocks, their dead eyes looking nowhere. I search for my mother's face, needing to look into her eyes one last time. If I am lucky enough to see Mama, I will close my eyes once we've driven by.

It is Mama's face I will keep as my last image.

I suck long cold breaths in through my nose and mouth, filling my lungs with air.

My tongue tastes of lead. I wonder...should I breathe in quickly when the gas pours out of the shower nozzle or should I hold my breath and in those extras twelve seconds remember Mama's face? I must decide quickly. I wonder what little cousin Effie did with her breath three months ago when she and her mother were gassed. How long does it take poison to fill the lungs of a tiny eleven-year-old ballerina?

"Did you write this, Doompshling?" Dina asks.

"Of course, I wrote it," I replied. "Actually, with our recordings, you wrote this, Dina. I simply listened to you and moved my fingers across the keyboard."

"OK. Keep going."

"Do you like it so far?" I asked…so wanting her approval.

"Just keep reading," she replied.

The jeep moves forward through human despair. I inhale and practice holding my breath. We pass the road to the crematorium where ceaseless black smoke rises from the chimneys. Saying nothing, the officer drives past the ovens, further into a field. Terrified and confused, I stay mute. Finally, he parks and tells me to get out and walk.

It is then I realize I will be shot. I pray he shoots me quickly with one bullet to my heart. I don't want him to shoot me in the head in case Mama ever finds me in that field. She must see my face as she knows it. She can pretend I am sleeping.

I follow the officer's stride through short grass and in the distance there is a bent figure covered by black cloth. I saw only his legs. As we get closer, I see the covered figure is leaning over a wooden box camera. In front of the lens a gypsy man poses.

His dark lifeless eyes stare straight ahead.

The man comes out from under the black cloth, turns to the officer and says, "Is she the one who painted the mural?" I stare at the officer hoping he will somehow protect me. I crouch behind his uniformed body using him as my shield.

He answers, "Yes, sir, she is."

The man considers my face and asks me directly, "Can you replicate human skin tones with your paint?"

I look at the ground and say, "Yes, sir. I can."

"Can you get the color more true, better than Technicolor film?"

"I can try," I answer.

The man nods to the officer who salutes him and that is all.

125

Soon I will learn that the man is Dr. Josef Mengele, the Angel of Death. And soon I will be forced to become his official artist, painting portraits of Roma, the Gypsies, for his research, proving these beautiful people are, according to Dr. Mengele, 'inferior to the supreme Aryan race.' Soon, I will be in a surgical theatre, painting a beating human as the Monster Mengele places it on the table where I sit with my sketch pad and palette of crude paints he bought for me. I will do these things because if I don't, I will be gassed.

Dina got up, went to the stove and took two brownies out of the pan. She put them on a white china plate and set it in front of me, refilled my coffee, sat down, and said, "OK." She said, "We should keep going."

I took that as high praise. "These are your best brownies ever, Dina," I exclaimed.

"Doomschpatz," came her reply.

The Pilot

Please buckle up. We are in for the ride of our lives.
– John Powell, Pilot and my dearest friend.

"You should get on OkCupid," my therapist said.
"What's that?" I replied.
"An online dating service."
"Are you on crack, Jane? I'm not doing that. Online dating is for losers!"
"Really? I met my husband on OkCupid and we had some kids." She smiled.

Two months later, on OkCupid, I met John. John called the dating site The OK Corral.

He responded to my brief profile which read: *Me in three: 'Petite, passionate, peripatetic.' Have well stamped passport and a sturdy Nikon.*

We met one week later at Cafe Gratitude in Larchmont Village in Hollywood.
I sat in my car applying lipstick. I saw who I thought was John walking to the restaurant. He's slim and handsome with silver hair cut short. His profile is strong. Dressed in a navy blue jacket and a grey scarf he looked European. I arrived at the restaurant and John wasn't there. A fat guy was. Turns out John was in the loo. I walked across the parking lot and pretended to look in the store windows. When I saw him, I called out, "John?" We dashed to each other like that shampoo commercial! Without a beat, John kissed me on my lips. Softly.

"You're perfect!" he said.

John's first words to me. Like he was assessing a Ferrari.

John was from Johannesburg and Cape Town, South Africa. I swooned at his accent. And if that wasn't sexy enough, he was a pilot! He was a private pilot flying for Elton John, Disney, and the Royal Family of Jordan: King Abdullah, Queen Rania, and the Princesses. Once John flew the Princesses to the Sultan of Brunei's summer palace for a birthday party for his daughter!

We walked hand in hand to the hostess desk. "Your usual table, Mr. Powell?" the young lady asked.

John replied, "Yes."

What the fuck? Is this guy holding auditions? He admitted that OkCupid is a numbers game.

"I've seen thirty women this month (!). I schedule lunch and dinner," John said.

That's weird! I thought.

"Judy, I have a dinner date here tomorrow. I don't want to see her. I want to close this deal with you. But to be a gentleman, I must."

OK. I think. *This guy is ethical.*

John ordered. I asked him to decide for me. I had wine. He didn't. I discovered he never drank alcohol, did drugs, or smoked.

John said, "So. You did *Castaway*! Tom Hanks and the basketball, right?"

Clearly, John didn't watch films. Stupidly, John had googled me and had seen some of my television interviews for my films. So there was little discovery.

"Tom had a volleyball. We shot that in Fiji. We crashed the FedEx plane on stage twenty-seven at Paramount," I announced.

Holding hands, we melded before our entrees arrived and stayed together for twelve years.

In short order, John became my emotional architect. I relied on him too much. John would come to me when he parked his jet. He'd arrive at my apartment at three am. I loved grilling him about his trips. Who did he fly with? Who were his passengers? What did the flight assistant serve him for dinner? What does the APU do? What was the most gorgeous place he saw from the cockpit? Answer: Aurora Borealis.

"Was flying sexy?"

"Fuck no. Just tedious."

"Bullshit!" I said. "How about takeoff and wheels down?"

"OK," admitted John, "not sexy but great if you get a good landing. It was typical to have two wheels down at one hundred and eighty miles per hour."

"Did you have good landings?" I said.

"Often."

My codependency killed us. I watched him constantly to make sure he was OK.

Did he need anything? Was he upset with me about anything, real or imagined? Was the broccoli steamed to his liking? If not, how could I change to please him? Exhausting really. For both of us.

After twelve years together, we broke up. John remains one of my dearest friends. I'd take a bullet for him. I'm so grateful he is forever in my life.

When I began my career, I was running warp speed to get away from myself. Now I run toward the woman I've become: a casting director, a writer, a romantic, a sister, a dear friend, and a trapeze artist.

Through Casting Glances, I've discovered that even though I'm single, I'm enough. I'm living happily ever after...*just like in the movies.*

End